UK Hip-Hop, Grime and 1

Young people in London have contributed to the production of a distinctively British rap culture. This book moves beyond accounts of hip-hop's marginality and shows, with an examination of the production, dissemination, and use of rap in London, how this cultural form plays an important role in the everyday lives of young Londoners and the formation of identities. Through in-depth interviews with a range of leading and emerging rap artists, close analysis of rap music tracks, and over two years of ethnographic research of London's UK hip-hop and grime scenes, Bramwell examines how black and white urban youths use rap to come together to explore their creative abilities. By combining these methodological approaches in the development of a critical participant observation, the book reveals how the collaborative work of these urban youths produced these politically significant subcultures, through which they resist unfair and illegitimate policing practices and attempt to develop their economic autonomy in a city marred by immense social and economic inequalities.

Richard Bramwell is a Research Associate at the University of Cambridge.

Routledge Advances in Ethnography

**Edited by Dick Hobbs, University of Essex, and
Geoffrey Pearson, Goldsmiths' College, University of London**

Ethnography is a celebrated, if contested, research methodology that offers unprecedented access to people's intimate lives, their often hidden social worlds, and the meanings they attach to these. The intensity of ethnographic fieldwork often makes considerable personal and emotional demands on the researcher, while the final product is a vivid human document with personal resonance impossible to recreate by the application of any other social science methodology. This series aims to highlight the best, most innovative ethnographic work available from both new and established scholars.

UK Hip-Hop, Grime and the City

The Aesthetics and Ethics of London's Rap Scenes

Richard Bramwell

Routledge
Taylor & Francis Group

LONDON AND NEW YORK

First published 2015 by Routledge

2 Park Square, Milton Park, Abingdon, Oxfordshire OX14 4RN
711 Third Avenue, New York, NY 10017

Routledge is an imprint of the Taylor & Francis Group, an informa business

First issued in paperback 2018

Library of Congress Cataloging-in-Publication Data

Bramwell, Richard, 1977–
    UK hip-hop, grime and the city : the aesthetics and ethics of London's rap
scenes / by Richard Bramwell.
        pages cm. — (Routledge advances in ethnography ; 14)
    Includes bibliographical references and index.
    1. Rap (Music)—Social aspects—England—London. I. Title.
    ML3918.R37B73 2015
    782.42164909421—dc23   2015002414

ISBN: 978-0-415-81238-2 (hbk)
ISBN: 978-1-138-31917-2 (pbk)

Typeset in Sabon
by Apex CoVantage, LLC

For Jane and Caius.

Contents

Acknowledgements

This book would not have been possible without the support of a number of people. I owe a special debt to Paul Gilroy for his generous advice and guidance during my doctoral studies through to the completion of this book. I would like to thank Fran Tonkiss and Dick Hobbs for their considered criticism as the fieldwork developed and Anne-Marie Fortier and Angela McRobbie for their advice on the publication of this research. Thanks to Jade Cummings and Dhanveer Singh Brar for reading early drafts of the book and providing valuable criticism. Thanks also to Antonia Dawes for her careful proof reading and feedback. Dhanveer Singh Brar, Omar El-Khairy, Shoshone Johnson, and Malcolm James enabled the ideas that provided the germs for this study to be cultivated within a spirit of friendship and critical exchange. Thanks also to Molly Crawford, Rosa Padfield, Jordan Channer, and Freya El Baz. I am grateful to Sukina and Muneera, both of Poetic Pilgrimage, and to Pariz 1 for participating in the research. Funding for this study was provided by the Arts and Humanities Research Council and the London School of Economics and Political Science.

Shout outs to Afrikan Boy, Dexplicit, Excalibah, JJ, Jeff, Klayze, Possessed, Reain, Seeker, Skirmish, Slik D, and Ty.

Universal Music Publishing Limited/Notting Hill Music (UK) Limited.
All rights for Hero Music Ltd. in the U.S. and Canada administered by Universal—Songs of Polygram International, Inc.
All rights for Notting Hill Music (UK) Ltd. in the U.S. and Canada administered by Notting Hill Music Inc.
All Rights Reserved. International Copyright Secured. Reprinted by permission of Hal Leonard Corporation, Music Sales Limited and Notting Hill Music Inc.

CASH IN MY POCKET

Words and Music by Mark Daniel Ronson, Richard Kyle Cowie and Daniel Paul Merriweather
© Copyright 2008 BMG VM Music Ltd and Marlin Publishing Pty Ltd.
All Rights for BMG VM Music Ltd administered by BMG Rights Management (US) LLC
All Rights for Marlin Publishing Pty Ltd administered by Universal Music Publishing Limited.
All Rights Reserved. Used by Permission.
Reprinted by permission of Hal Leonard Corporation and Music Sales Limited.

Introduction

This book is about rap music produced in London. The widespread popularity of hip-hop and the emergence of grime as a distinct London sound highlight the importance of examining the role that rap plays in contemporary Britain. With the entry of artists such as the So Solid Crew, Roll Deep, Wretch 32, Tinie Tempah, and Chipmunk into the top of the UK charts, and Dizzee Rascal's performance as part of the opening ceremony of the London 2012 Olympic Games, the rap music of this city has entered the mainstream of British life. However, there are currently no other books that examine the production of rap in the United Kingdom and the role that it plays in the formation of young people's identities. This book addresses that gap in hip-hop studies by examining how young people in London have contributed to the production of a distinctively British rap culture. Through an in-depth examination of the production, dissemination, and use of rap in this city, I aim to move beyond accounts of hip-hop's marginality and examine how this cultural form plays an important role in the everyday lives of young Londoners.

I was compelled to begin working on a book-length project during the celebrations of hip-hop's 30th anniversary. While this was an important milestone in the development of rap as the most popular poetic form in the world today, these celebrations emphasised the role of America's commercial recording industry and largely ignored the role of rap and hip-hop in everyday life. At that point rap had been an ordinary feature of English life for over 35 years. There is increasing recognition of the need to direct critical attention to rap music outside of the US (Mitchell 2001). The focus of existing studies of rap on American hip-hop culture relies upon categories of race that cannot be directly translated into the multiethnic context of this English city, in which patterns of segregation are less spatially marked (Hall 2012). Specific histories of racism and patterns of migration have produced distinctive black cultures in the US. By shifting focus from American hip-hop to London's rap scenes, I aim to explore how forms of social identification across and outside of racial categories are constructed through rap in a European city with very different patterns of racism and economic segregation to those of New York and other cities in the US.

London's black popular culture cannot be properly understood in terms of the localisation of globalised US hip-hop (Bennett 1999). The city's contemporary rap scenes trace their routes through Africa and the Caribbean, as well as the US. They are produced by artists whose experiences of migration are often unrelated to that of the Windrush generation. The exploration of identities and relationships in rap songs, by artists such the Sierra Leonian Skirmish of Rhyme Asylum or the British-Nigerian Afrikan Boy, work with and against the self-representation of artists whose relation to Africa is mediated through Caribbean culture. The adoption of rap as a popular mode of expression amongst white English youths, as well as the migration of British hip-hop artists, such as Monie Love, to the US, are indications of the complex patterns of identification and migration that produce London's rap cultures. Although the way in which rap is appropriated by British-Asians, used to construct their identities and address their concerns, is an important part of the role that black culture plays in Britain (Kim 2012), I am unable to attend to those issues in this space. Instead of dealing with the appropriation of black culture by other ethnic minority groups, I examine how rap is employed in social spaces dominated (but not exclusively occupied) by young black people and how its appropriation by white, working-class youths can be seen as a politically significant aspect of the mainstreaming of black culture in the United Kingdom.

This book was also borne out of a sense of frustration with scholarship that either looked at rap solely as a poetic form that could be reduced to a text or, alternatively, that approached hip-hop exclusively as a set of social and economic relations. These approaches, in their different ways, failed to account for the important connections between the economic activities, social relations, and the formal qualities of rap as a performed oral genre. I wanted to develop a methodological approach to rap music that more closely approximated the experience of its oral poetry while engaging with the social practices through which that pleasure is produced. While it is important to acknowledge rap's literary value, the methods through which literary studies approach this poetic form need to undergo rigorous critical attention. Although aspects of rap may be amenable to textual analysis, it is important to emphasise that this is an oral poetic form. The performative dimension of the rapper's work and its role in the production of identification through the body are important aspects of this art form. By drawing on a combination of methods from the social sciences and the humanities, this book contributes to the construction of an approach to this art form that is able to address rap on its own terms. Through this approach it is also possible to engage with the social and political significance of this black cultural form.

Finally, the enduring presence of rap cultures in the United Kingdom, over several generations, has significant implications for the consideration of British and English identities. Rap plays a significant role in cultivating habits of living with difference and sustaining radical passions for a more substantively inclusive democracy. The immediate (and resolutely parochial) aim of this study is to draw attention to the depth of England's black culture by exploring how rap has become an ordinary feature of everyday life in one particular city. Its broader aim is to commence a reappraisal of the role of rap in Europe. Through a focus on the UK hip-hop and grime scenes in London, I want to highlight the importance of attending to the social, aesthetic, and economic practices that constitute the rap scenes of other European cities. While London operates as an important junction point in black Atlantic culture, the rap cultures of Birmingham, Nottingham, Paris, Marseilles, Milan, Naples, and Malmö have their own local histories and specific social, geographic, and economic configurations. This art form provides a privileged entry point into the production of translocal identifications in the practice of everyday urban life and an important means through which to engage with the construction of alternative European identities.

1 'Revolution of a Next Kind'
Building Black London from the Bottom

Reain tells me that he spells his stage name a particular way for the purpose of putting two words together, 'and two meanings together.' His discussion of this name contrasts with what he refers to as his 'given name.' While there is nothing in our conversation to suggest any discomfort with the name given him by his family, '. . . the name of a king, brap!,' the description he provides of the process of constructing another name, appropriate to himself, reveals a considered approach to the identity that he inhabits as a rapper. 'You know you've got reign sovereign r, e, i, g, n, and you've got rain weather, and that's what, basically, I'm trying to bring across.' Although he does not make the connection more explicit, his valorisation of an aspect of his given name, related to monarchy, may be associated with his efforts to communicate the idea '[not] that I'm better than anyone, but just in a sense that I think . . . that anyone has a potential to be a king. Within their own right.' This sense of Reain's neologism is combined with another, which he considers to be 'a bit more aggy: "Right I'm pissing down on people". And that's a bit more where the battle and rugged element comes into my style.' By combining these words and meanings Reain fashions a sense of himself that incorporates a street ruggedness with a sense of dignity that the working-class, black Englishman believes is accessible to anyone: 'whether you're sweeping the roads or whether you're sat on a throne.' He took this name at about 16 or 17 years old, after listening to his elder brother's rap music as a child, and rapping from the age of 15. As one of many genres of music that were played in his home, rap provided him with valuable cultural resources through which he has constructed his adult identity.

Through participating in rap music cultures young Londoners develop a sense of themselves. This sense includes awareness of their place in the world, the city they inhabit, and the relations with others through which their life experiences are structured. Rapping becomes an important part of the production of particular modes of urban living through various forms of play and the exploration of the relations that are constitutive of this verbal art form. This productive activity occurs in a variety of sites, including the home, school, and youth clubs. The acquisition of the linguistic skills that distinguish one as a rapper enables young people to achieve social recognition, to cultivate forms of self-esteem, and develop the means to attain economic and social aspirations. In the act of rapping they appropriate means to represent themselves and the urban world they inhabit, both to themselves and others. As young rappers develop, their interests and investments in this art form may enlarge to include, not only pleasure and social recognition for their skills, but also concern for the organisation of social life, and the socioeconomic and political forces that structure their lives and the reproduction of their culture.

These interests and concerns are developed through a variety of processes, including copying rappers on the radio, writing lyrics in the bedroom, clashing with other rappers in a circle at school, and practicing what one artist described as the 'lost art' of freestyling. Rapping and playing with products made through or with rap contribute to the construction of distinctive forms of intersubjectivity, collective identifications, and social skills. Reain's combination of the vulgar with the dignified in his identity reveals a concern with self-possession. He refers to a Nas lyric, 'blood of a slave, heart of a King,' that he heard some time after giving himself the name 'Reain.' In relating this lyric to his name, he indicates how the themes and values that circulate in this culture affirm and express his own sentiments. By explaining this aspect of his identity through another's lyrics, Reain also demonstrates how one's sense of self is nurtured and extended through participation in rap cultures. The affirmation of his identity through rap and a reference to slavery is an important consideration in the study of contemporary life in the postcolonial city.

The circles formed in playgrounds and nightclubs across London can be seen as a refashioning of a vital component of slave culture and the premodern African forms upon which the slaves drew. In this reshaping, advanced technologies are combined with black cultural resources in the development of new aesthetic forms and intersubjective relations. This cultural and technological work contributes to the ongoing reconfiguration of the 'black public sphere' in contemporary London (Baker 1996).

This chapter considers the ethical relations and aesthetic forms produced by young people in their development as rap artists and in their construction of the city's rap scenes. It aims to explore some of the distinctive features that rap contributes to the formation of a black public sphere in contemporary London. My examination of the ethics and aesthetics of rap music cultures begins with a brief outline of the historical development of the city's rap tradition. I then turn to artists' recollections of their initial experiences of this cultural form. Through these recollections of cultural acquisition and development, I consider the relationships formed in the production of rap and the shared time and space that rappers inhabit. Following this I analyse how rap's aesthetic qualities are shaped by the social relations through which it is produced. Through this discussion of the relations between aesthetic and social forms, I aim to highlight how the use of technology in the contemporary, black public sphere distinguishes

London's rap cultures from those produced during slavery and in the post-emancipation Caribbean.

Following these preliminary discussions, I move on to an examination of how rap is appropriated by urban youths in the production of their social identities and how these cultural practitioners contribute to the construction of the UK hip-hop and grime scenes. This analysis attends to the inclination of social subjects towards particular dispositions through participation in rap cultures. It also engages with the collaborative processes through which technology and labour are employed in the construction of London's black public sphere. Through this engagement I highlight the proximity of those cultural spaces to specific contexts of urban dwelling. I then return to the connection between technology and ethical relations in the black public sphere, in order to examine the convergence of factors that came about in the production of grime music in London. Following this, I discuss the significance of the intergenerational reproduction of the city's rap cultures both inside and outside of the family structure. The social recognition gained through rapping is an important aspect of young people's social development, as well as mature artists' economic aspirations. I therefore conclude with a consideration of the social significance of the adaptation of this cultural practice to the conditions of postcolonial London.

'I DROP JEWELS': APPROPRIATING A CULTURAL INHERITANCE

The participation of youths from a variety of ethnic backgrounds in contemporary London's rap scenes is testament to the tenacity of this art form. The presence of a culture of rap in this city is, certainly in part, related to the global dominance of American popular culture. However, it is necessary to bring to the fore the significance of alternate routes that have contributed to the production of London's black music cultures. In particular, I want to highlight the significance of Caribbean migration to the formation of this city's rap culture. Prince Buster's work in the Jamaican popular music culture of the 1960s, which built on the practice of DJ toasting (Hebdige 1993), may be seen to anticipate the development of rap. Although hip-hop is considered to have its origins in the South Bronx, Kool DJ Herc is widely recognised as one of the culture's 'pioneers' (Rose 1994; Potter 1995). Herc is credited with importing elements of the sound system culture that hip-hop is built upon from his native Jamaica. The historian Joseph Heathcott argues that 'ska and reggae provided important groundwork for . . . rap music, as island peoples brought the Jamaican sound system, the MC . . . and a vibrant dancehall culture to the immigrant neighborhoods of urban America' (2003: 185). The migration of large numbers of West Indians to postwar England produced a similar development of black Atlantic culture, laying the 'groundwork' for the transnational flow of sound system culture to Britain. In their production of 'some of the most important British reggae recordings in the late 1970s' Dennis Bovell and Linton Kwesi Johnson drew upon the same pool of Caribbean cultural resources as Kool Herc (Chambers 1985). Johnson's (1976) discussion of 'Jamaican Rebel Music' refers to the practice of dub-poetry, which forms a key historical link between black London's culture and its Atlantic routes:

> The 'dub-lyricist' is the dj turned poet. He intones his lyrics rather than sings them. Dub-lyricism is a new form of (oral) music-poetry, wherein the lyricist overdubs rhythmic phrases on to the rhythm background of a popular song. Dub-lyricists include poets like Big Youth, I Roy, U Roy, Dillinger, Shorty the President, Prince Jazzbo and others.

Johnson's own practice as a dub-poet signals the presence of this cultural tradition in the UK at least as far back as the period that saw hip-hop's 'birth' in New York during the 1970s. While the London Posse's recordings in the late 1980s and early 1990s contributed to a significant moment in the development of British hip-hop, by drawing on English, Caribbean, and American styles, Johnson's dub poetry can be seen as an antecedent to the laid-back flow of MCs such as Roots Manuva and Ghostpoet.

The dub-lyricist's expression of the memory of suffering during slavery and the continued unfreedoms to which blacks are subject may be usefully compared with Sterling Stuckey's discussion of slave culture and the 'ring shout.' Stuckey (1987) identified that slaves' lyrics were 'driven by complex percussive rhythms, and often give way to chants, whose repetition can have a hypnotic effect and contribute to the high religious purpose of possession.' This religious purpose was associated with the specific social, economic, and political position in which the slaves found themselves. The African rhythms that the slaves drew on were 'adapted, changed, and intensified by the tragic soul-life of the slaves' (DuBois 2000). While this culture has undergone considerable modification, many of its formal qualities have also been retained and refined. Stuckey's description of the slaves' lyrics bears similarities to what Adam Krims (2000) terms 'percussion effusive flow' in contemporary hip-hop culture. In considering the presence of this tradition in contemporary London, it is important to attend to the adaptations and transformations at work in this syncretic culture. Hesmondhalgh and Melville (2001) highlight that in the 1980s 'the United Kingdom already had an emancipatory black practice, a Caribbean derived cultural formation with music at its epicentre that fostered black expressivity and organised and channelled critiques of institutional racism and neocolonialism.' It was partly because of the presence of this syncretic youth culture that US hip-hop artists found a sympathetic audience in Britain. Within this distinctly multiethnic context English youths further adapted the materials of these rap cultures to their own purposes. The practice of rapping in London is not the result of a simple handing down of a finished culture, but part of an ongoing process of adapting and reworking cultural resources to the conditions in which practitioners find themselves.

Although the contexts of production may be significantly different, the association that London's youths have with rap music may indicate one of the key reasons for its historical longevity. Stuckey (1987) notes, in his discussion of the 'ring shout,' that 'Black youngsters were eager to "shout," forming themselves into a circle, singing and dancing at the slightest suggestion, assuring the perpetuation of important religious and artistic values of their people.' The appropriation of the ring shout in London may meet very different needs to those expressed in the slaves' song and dance, but the adaptation of the slave circle into cyphers and clashes by young Londoners suggests that it remains an important social practice through which they craft their adult identities. I argue that MCs and DJs also facilitate a collective experience, a practice that retains important links with the tradition of black expressive culture. For Johnson (1976), the dub-lyricist embodied 'the historical experience of the Jamaican masses':

> Through music, song and poetry, they give spiritual expression to their own inner beings, to their own experience. But in so doing, they are also giving spiritual expression to the collective experience of sufferation that is shared by all sufferers.

In the study of British rap it is necessary to examine how grime and UK hip-hop MCs employ their cultural resources in the production of alternative, oppositional interpretations of metropolitan life.

Following Houston Baker's (1996) critical reformulation of Habermas's public sphere as a plural space, I want to explore how rap culture contributes to the production of a vibrant, black public sphere in London. In contrast to the subjectivity formed through the consumption of the psychological novel from which, Habermas (1989) argues, the rational-critical public debate that characterised the bourgeois public sphere flowed, the antiphonic structure of rap prioritises the value of intersubjectivity. Kamau Brathwaite (1984) contrasts the Jamaican oral tradition with the written tradition of Western poetry, as a form of total expression:

> Reading is an isolated, individualistic expression. The oral tradition on the other hand demands not only the griot but the audience to complete the community: The noise and sounds that the maker makes are responded to by the audience and are returned to him. Hence we have the creation of a continuum where meaning truly resides.

In this total expression, voice, body movement, and gesture are combined with the materiality of sound in the production of an interpretative community. The consumption of literary texts emphasises a private subjectivity, and formed an important channel through which the culture of the dominant social group developed. By contrast, the *intersubjectivity* that structures the use of rap music by initiates of London's black culture is an essential component in the development of that culture and of its practitioners. The artistic forms and social values that are made and adapted in the subaltern, black public sphere can be seen to affirm important principles of commonality in contemporary London.

A TIME TO BE TOGETHER: THE ETHICS OF RAP

The sense of a common present forms the basis of my link between the aesthetics and ethics of rap music. In his discussion of convivial culture, Bourdieu (1984: 183) opposes the subjectivity that the petit bourgeois constructs by withdrawal into the home, with the 'being in the present' that is affirmed in the 'readiness to take advantage of the good times and take time as it comes.' He argues that this presence is 'in itself, an affirmation of solidarity with others.' I want to invest in the formal features of rap music an ethical value. These qualities may be observed in the forms of spontaneity, improvisation, recognition, and reciprocity that are employed in the city's black public sphere. They are influenced by historical and technological developments. In order to understand rap's role in the formation of identity in contemporary London, attention must be directed to how social, economic, technological, and political factors influence this cultural practice. Paul Willis highlights, in his discussion of grounded aesthetics, that 'there is a dramaturgy and poetics of everyday life, of social presence, encounter and event' (1990: 22). The ethics of play through which young Londoners signify their lived conditions are of central importance to the grounded aesthetics that I am attempting to outline here. The strategies of play and self-organisation that structure the subaltern public sphere can be usefully related to Bakhtin's discussion of the carnival grotesque.

> The carnivalesque crowd in the marketplace or in the streets is not merely a crowd. It is the people as a whole, but organized *in their own way*, the way of the people. It is outside and contrary to all existing forms of socio-economic and political organization, which is suspended for the time of the festivity.
>
> (Bakhtin 1984: 255, emphasis in the text)

The structure of contemporary London's black public sphere is not determined by the responses of slaves and colonised people to their conditions. However, the dispositions that are acquired through the practice of rapping incline subjects towards a particular orientation to the social world. As the challenges posed by that world change, each generation adapts the cultural resources that they inherit to deal with those conditions. Many of the themes employed in clashing are characteristic of the carnival grotesque:

> The body that figures in all the expressions of the unofficial speech of the people is the body that fecundates and is fecundated, that gives birth and is born, devours and is devoured, drinks, defecates, is sick and dying. In all languages there is a great number of expressions related to the genital organs, the anus and buttocks, the belly, the mouth and nose.
> (Bakhtin 1984: 319)

The use of vulgar language in London's UK hip-hop and grime scenes emphasises the material and bodily. Susan Buck-Morss reminds us that the 'original field of aesthetics is not art but reality—corporeal, material nature' (1992: 6). The grotesque aesthetic is adapted within these scenes to common goals and the present conditions of dwelling. Furthermore, Reain's reference to slavery suggests a lingering awareness of the value that the memory of racial terror may have in London's black public sphere. He employs this value in the service of dealing with his own situation as a working-class black man, possessing dignity with common values and interests.

There are a number of different styles of rap with various qualities in which pleasure is found by the young inhabitants of this city. The practice is associated with the development of friendships inside and outside of school. Beginning to rap is regarded as a form of play, frequently compared to football, and as something to do with friends: '[E]veryone was doing it' (Daz). It is also related by the city's youths to a feeling that is enjoyed and the desire to be the person who brings about that feeling in others. Above all it is considered by young artists to have been an ordinary part of growing up. Listening to rap music is a common feature in Britain's youth cultures. Whether via the radio, Internet, or purchased recordings, the use of recorded rap music is an essential component in London's rap cultures. Listening to records with friends, retracing the lyrics of a favourite artist, gathering around a radio at night, or MCing over a record as part of a bedroom set are just a few of the ways in which recorded music is used in the reproduction of black culture in the city. The forms of play through which young Londoners develop their understanding of black urban life can lead to a new sense of self.

MCs frequently contrast rapping at 15 or 16 with experiences of rapping that occurred earlier in childhood. Although MCing during one's midteens is occasionally described as something like a hobby, childhood rapping is seen as less 'serious' than the more practiced engagement with black culture that occurs during and following adolescence. The adoption of a name that is recognised amongst one's peer group or beyond is one of the ways in which participation in black urban culture transforms the lives of a substantial number of young people in the capital. UK hip-hop and grime artists refer to youth clubs as important sites for the development of their skills and spaces in which their admiration of MCs had been ignited. However, youth clubs are not usually places in which young people first begin to rap. The artistic skills and cultural competence required to be confident enough to perform in front of others are developed at home, in private or with friends. Less formally organised spaces such as parks, a wall in the local neighbourhood, or school corridors also provide opportunities to increase verbal facility.

Describing the scene in which his interest in rap music arose, DJ Excalibah recalls his friend's room in a house in Leyton. 'I remember us both sitting . . . listening to the album, like into what we thought were the wee hours, but I had to be home by nine so it wasn't that late. . . . And him trying to tell me why hip-hop was amazing.' The reconstruction of this event reveals one of the ordinary ways in which rap shapes experience. Excalibah's recollection of a discrepancy between his perception of time and the temporality by which his life was generally governed indicates how this engagement with rap music modified his experience of time's passing. Engaging with rap produces a shift in temporal perspective, as well as the development of interpretative techniques:

> I think it was Blackstreet I got into first, and it was like one song 'You Blow My Mind' which had the rap on it.—[breaks into rap with a companion:] 'Check baby, check baby, one two, one two'—and I was like 'What's he saying, what's he saying?' and he was like 'Oh it's rap.' And he played me more rap which was the Fugees. Then I got into Foxy Brown 'cause she had the song with Blackstreet, then Biggie, then Little Kim, and the acts—Jay-Z—all the acts that were big at the time.

In describing the everyday moment in which he first identified an interest in rap music, Excalibah demonstrates how this further developed, through a chain of references to other artists. The manner of his recollection also reveals the power of the rappers' performative utterances. Breaking into rhyme with his companion foregrounds the role of rap music in affirming social relations and the invocation of a convivial 'being in the present.' Craig Mack's repetition and rhythmic play on 'You Blow My Mind' evokes a response that not only involves repetition but a shift in position, from that of a listener to the enunciative position of the rapper. In doing so the temporality of that play is reinvoked in the present.

In contrast to Excalibah's narrative, Daz[1] describes asking his father's friend to make a mixtape because he was fascinated by turntables:

> He was the first person that I knew that had decks. He was playing House music, I never liked House music. But I so wanted to get into music that I used to lie to him and say 'my Dad wants you to make him

a tape.' . . . 'So can I come up there and pick tunes that I think he will like, and you put it on a tape, and I'll give it to him.' And boom! . . . I used to go in and go through his records, I didn't know what any of the tunes were, but he used to say 'alright then' and I used to pick the tunes, and he used to play them and mix them all together, and that was my first recollection of getting involved in being a DJ . . . I never used to give it to my Dad, and I never used to listen to the tape, 'cause I never liked House music. But it was me seeing them decks spinning around, and him mixing it, and me being intrigued.

The shift in focal point, from subject, to object (the spinning decks), and back to subject, dramatises the process of identification that led to Daz's career in music. Both Excalibah and Daz's narratives emphasise the inter-subjectivity that their interests in rap music were built upon. In spite of this early interest in DJing, Daz first productively engaged with rap music as an MC, at school and in his friends' homes:

When we was 14 or 15 and that, there was one guy that I knew . . . and he used to call himself MC Element. And he had Soundlab decks and I used to invite my friends 'round to his house. We wasn't even called anything then. And we used to go to his house—'cause I used to buy jungle records those times—and we used to go and do our sets. . . . We used to MC, me and him, and [my friend] used to DJ or whatever. And that's where the progression came from.

There is a reference to a social form here that is a fundamental compo-nent in the reproduction of contemporary, black-British culture: the 'bed-room set.' Daz's reference to Element's self-identification is followed by the statement that the group of friends that assembled to practice their artistic techniques did not have a name at that time. They had not acquired a col-lective identity that they felt required naming. Nevertheless, Daz's practice of MCing over jungle records enabled the cultivation of important cultural competences. The bedroom set produces a form of social organisation that requires a division of labour between the DJ and MCs. It also employs an intersubjective linguistic play that is structured by the temporality of the selected recordings. Rapping with other MCs over the rhythm of records selected by the DJ, in these organisations, is an important part of the pro-cess of developing as a rap artist. The absence of a name for the group (in contrast to later associations in which Daz was a member) reveals the inter-mediate position of bedroom sets. This position is made particularly distinct as a result of the individuals within that group adopting names that identify them as particular types of cultural practitioners. The bedroom set may be described as a private association of members who have made public their identification with rap music culture, whose primary purpose is to develop the skills required to reproduce that culture.

COMMON CULTURE: THE AESTHETICS OF RAP

The skills employed in the bedroom set are not only developed in private spaces. The public spaces of the school, street, and local parks are used in order to practice and explore these linguistic techniques. Through that exploration these spaces are, to a greater or lesser degree, transformed. Indeed, it is in the organisation of space that is not one's own that personal development is mediated and oriented towards social development. Seeker,[2] now in his 30s, recalls playing in the park with friends during the early 1990s, prior to the period that Daz describes above:

> [We would be] freestyling, or trying to freestyle I would call it now. . . . Someone would be beat-boxing the wackest beat-box, just [beat-boxes], just you know just beat-boxing—just us chilling, sitting down. And it was about who would come out with the freshest rhyme as well, at that moment in time. And that was encouraging, because it sometimes inspired lyrics, to see who could bring something next or something new to the table.

The friendly competition within the group encouraged participants to practice privately, in order to improve their verbal skills. In addition to the different uses of public and private space (private for writing, oriented to performance in public space with, and for, other practitioners), the use of other materials, such as video, is further oriented towards this intersubjective play through participation in black cultural production:

> . . . and around that time as well was the movie *House Party* . . . you had Kid who wasn't exactly the most popular of students but he had been practicing, crafting his art, and now bringing it forward to get that recognition with it, that's how it felt for us back then, that was the early birth of the love for hip-hop.

Willis argues that video 'has unique characteristics which change the nature of viewing in important ways':

> It also gives viewers more control over the way they watch and over the materials of their own symbolic work. They can speed scan the whole thing, skip sequences they don't like, repeat one's they do, slow the action down, and freeze a single frame on the screen. By allowing a more active relationship to the screen than is possible with conventional television viewing, these facilities open up new possibilities for symbolic creativity and begin to blur the line between consumption and production.
>
> (Willis 1990: 39)

Through this active relation to cultural material, young Londoners adapt these resources to their own needs. Like Seeker, Ty recalls using the *House*

Party video. In his case it was employed in the development of his repertoire of dance moves. Their use of video identifies how communicative technologies are employed in the process of vernacular identity formation. Seeker's experience contrasts with Daz's, both in the use of space (the selection of a particular space, as well as how it is used) and in the technological resources through which his engagement with rap developed. However, American hip-hop videos and British jungle records have both been employed as raw materials in the production of rap in London. The bedroom sets organised at MC Element's home are identified by Daz as enabling a 'progression.' The use of technology, association of friends, and the practicing of linguistic skills are important elements in this process.

Through his participation in rap culture Reain came to know and be affiliated with Rhyme Asylum. The crew's comments about their development within the UK hip-hop scene bears important testimony to the subjective feelings that are produced through rapping and the effect of different forms of social organisation on those feelings. In their discussion of the open mic events that they used to attend at the Deal Real record shop, Possessed and Skirmish emphasise its importance in the development of their skills and the feeling that it gave them:

> SKIRMISH: I used to love that man, the buzz, it was the illest feeling.
> POSSESSED: Yeah it was amazing, then I went every Friday for like three and a half years. Getting—doing the same thing. And that's how—yeah—where I learnt everything.
> SKIRMISH: That's when you start learning your skills innit, you're learning how to perform in front of a crowd, what the crowd reacts to. When you'd come up with a new verse and you'd spit it and get a good response: That's a good Friday man. You're like 'yeah.'
> POSSESSED: It would make you write as well because you'd feel like a bit of a knob if you'd been there for weeks and you'd spit the same verse.

These comments bring together themes of subjective feeling, cultural practice, and collective affirmation that are important aspects of the social production of the aura of London's rap cultures. In addition to the open mic events, the crew discuss cyphers and freestyling as distinct forms through which MCs were organised in the practice of their art. The open mic events embody the democratic principle of allowing anyone the opportunity to take the mic when the feeling strikes. However, this principle is structured and operates in a manner that is distinct to that found in the cypher.

Asserting that the cypher is 'fundamental' to an MC's development, Reain identifies a particular competitiveness as an important feature that distinguishes this form of rapping: 'When you're in a cypher, and it's other MCs—so you know—well the expectation is these guys are on exactly the same wave length as me, so I can't slip things by them. So they'll clock on and if I'm shit . . . you're not gonna get a pat on the back or anything.' He emphasises the high levels of skill demanded by the close competition, in which the rapper works no longer as a member of a crew but instead as part of a cypher. This involves elated highs, as well as low moments when one is found lacking:

REAIN: But its in a subtle way—no one's gonna come up to you and
            say 'ah, you're shit bruv.' . . . Yeah, you'll get a polite pat.
POSSESSED: Or the cut off 'Yo' . . .
REAIN: So you'll be rapping and someone will just jump in on
            your verse.

In contrast to the ongoing work that brings together the members of a crew, rappers who form a cypher work with and against one another in temporary formations directed to brief elevated highs. This sociocultural formation incorporates a competitiveness that is unsparing of the ego of those that are deemed to not meet the quality that other members of the cypher expect:

Its just a really good feeling and sense of camaraderie as well. You know you're all MCs together, you're all just rapping. Everyone's catching joke off it, and everyone's feeling everyone. Well not everyone really—you know you've got your shit guys. But you know—you know you need everything to make the recipe work.

(Possessed)

Reain and Possessed draw attention to the elements of spontaneity that are combined with the self-governing freedom of these 'temporary autonomous zones' (Bey 1985): 'They [cyphers] were my favourite part but its kind of like, where there is no scene you don't really get an opportunity and they're a lot better when they're spontaneous.' The festive quality of the cypher is an important component of the aura of this rap culture. The double-edged freedom embodied in the relative uncertainty of the timing of the events themselves and the self-legislation through which they are internally organised contrasts with the orderliness of open mic events. However, the timing of the events is related to the organisation of other aspects of the UK hip-hop scene. The cyphers that these artists participated in frequently occurred outside organised events.

The lack of opportunity for cyphering is related to the stagnation of the UK hip-hop scene. With spaces such as Deal Real gone, artists focus on other means through which to develop themselves. The contrast between the spontaneous cyphers and open mic events reveals a difference in the formal arrangement of space and the participants in it. It also highlights the necessity of institutions such as youth clubs and record shops like Deal Real to the development of a healthy rap scene. The contrast between freestyling and using verses memorised from previously written material draws further attention to the process of rapping and the 'texture' of the event. While either 'writtens' or 'freestyles' may be performed in a cypher, freestyling was identified by Reain and Possessed variously as 'the most creative part of hip-hop,' a 'lost art,' and the 'rawest form' of rapping. This is especially the case when a rapper refers to something spatially present in order to draw attention to the fact that he is freestyling. The mode of rapping 'from the top of the head' (which emphasises the 'happening right there, at that moment') can be compared to the free speech of Bakhtin's festive marketplace: 'A lot of the stuff, as long as you are freestyling, isn't gonna get said again. And its special to that moment, and every time you do it, it's something new and you can surprise yourself.' The originality of capturing a moment in this form involves the inventive use of free language and the privileging of the present, in contrast to the composition of written verses that are repeatedly honed before memorisation for performance.

Prewritten lyrics may, however, be used to support the build-up of extemporaneous rapping. In one of Afrikan Boy's videos published on YouTube, 'Afrikan Boy 3Style 4Captian TB TV,' he raps, 'On the bus my Oyster card goes "ding de diing de ding ding." ' These words form part of a lyric written in response to the introduction of this technology during his time at college: 'It realises that I am Afrikan Boy so when it beeps, it beeps that tune.' The imagined scenario of the bus recognising him, by responding to him swiping his card through playing a tune he had become engrossed in at the time of writing, is rapped along with a number of other '16 bar' lyrics in the production of an oral mash-up for this video. The mixture of memorised lyrics was also used as the basis for extemporised rapping by Excalibah and his crew during their development as artists: 'What you normally do is start with something that you've written, and once you forget a piece of it, start making it up until you have to stop, until you've gone rubbish.' The lyrical content of Afrikan Boy's freestyle video was composed through an openness to developments around him, and the putting together of incongruous elements to produce their humour. His mash-up of memorised lyrics involves a shift of consciousness. This movement is further developed in the process that Excalibah identifies as a type of fabrication, combined with forgetting.

In contrast to Excalibah, Reain's statement that he began freestyling prior to writing lyrics reveals that the primacy of orality persists within this culture. Reain points out that skilled freestylers may enter the cypher with a phrase such as 'I'm coming off the top' to draw attention to their practice of rapping lyrics extemporaneously. Although Reain and Possessed both particularly value the spontaneity of freestyling within cyphers and the state of consciousness that is attained through this form of social organisation, they also emphasise the need to practice in order to develop this skill. Possessed practices every day and is comfortably able to freestyle for over an hour. This skill is maintained through practicing with Reain and, alternatively, when playing tunes alone, beginning to freestyle when he is 'feeling the beat.'

The regular practicing of freestyle rapping, the value that is given to spontaneity, and the resultant uniqueness of the lyrics that are produced highlight the ontological status of rap as an event. In London's rap cultures, the skills exercised in producing these events are prioritised over the existence of a textual artefact. These skills include linguistic facility, the ability to adapt to a beat, and to draw upon immediately surrounding material. In developing an outline of the aesthetics of London-based rap, I wish to attend to the dialogical relationship between the rapper and recorded material (whether these be written lyrics, CDs, or MP3s). It is also necessary to connect the shift in consciousness, or forgetting, that Excalibah draws attention to with the 'shit' that is discarded in cyphers as aspects of the ground upon which the aesthetic experience of freestyling and cyphering work. The rap music that is used in the composition of prewritten verses, or as the basis for the practice of freestyling, is transformed from a finished product into the raw materials of these processes. Afrikan Boy's video presents a moment when disparate lyrics are employed in the production of an aural bricolage. Further to this, Excalibah's identification of the process of 'forgetting' as an important moment in building a freestyle can be paralleled with the cutting-off of an MC's contribution to a cypher in order to allow the cypher itself to develop. Although prewritten verses may be employed within the cypher, Reain and Possessed emphasise an innate spontaneity, cultivated through ongoing practice, in their valorisation of freestyling as rapping in its 'most raw form.'

The development of this form of aesthetic experience amongst rappers through a combination of other artists' beats in the production of written material, the reconfiguration of that prewritten material as the ground to begin working upon, the drawing upon material presently at hand, and the placing of other material out of mind in a spontaneous performance is important in the consideration of the manner in which MCs offer their lyrics to their audiences. Willis emphasises that ' "messages" are not now so much "sent" and "received" as *made* in reception, often as a result of, or at least appearing in the space made free and usable by the operation of grounded aesthetics' (1990: 135). The practice of developing linguistic skills through a variety of cultural and technological resources highlights how rap's grounded aesthetics are produced in the reworking of meaning in the black public sphere.

Although freestyling may draw attention to the immanence that Kamau Brathwaite identifies as key to the development of vernacular language, the practice of rapping in contemporary London is fashioned through advanced technologies. This condition, which can be apprehended through both the form and theme of Afrikan Boy's freestyle, sharply contrasts with those conditions experienced by the impoverished Caribbean people that Brathwaite describes:

> And this *total expression* comes about because people be in the open air, because people live in conditions of poverty ('unhouselled') because

they come from a historical experience where they had to rely on their very *breath* rather than on paraphernalia like books and museums and machines. They had to depend on *immanence*, the power with-in themselves, rather than the technology outside themselves.

(Brathwaite 1984: 19, emphasis in the text)

In addition to the power within themselves, contemporary rappers draw upon advanced digital technologies in their verbal expression. Developments in mobile phones played a particularly important role in contemporary London's black culture. The playing and exchange of music via mobile phone facilitates the growth and reproduction of London's contemporary rap cultures. This mode of mobile digital exchange operates alongside comparatively fixed modes, such as those provided through desktop-based tools like MSN.

The growth of this cultural economy is inseparable from a series of technological developments over the last 20 years. Although Daz and Ty recall early experiments with tape and vinyl, Seeker's use of a minidisc player as a compressor, connected to a computer, identifies his early participation in rap as coinciding with the shift from analogue to digital media and processes. The declining cost of home computers during the late 1990s and first decade of the new millennium was a significant step in broadening access to information technology. Willis states that '[o]f the 33 per cent of UK 16–24 year olds living in a household possessing a micro in 1987, most were in affluent homes' (1990: 40). It was possible to purchase a laptop in 2010 for less than £250, or a PC for less than £200, whereas 20 years prior a far less powerful personal computer could cost over £2000. The availability of 'cracked' copies of programmes such as Fruityloops, which were freely distributed amongst young rap music producers, increased the opportunity for amateurs to begin to produce music on cheap home computers. Groups of young rappers would gather in the home of one of their number to develop the technological skills required to produce digital rap music. Furthermore, the arrival of cheap CDRs increased the ease of duplication and distribution for both consumers and producers. The ability to use one form of media at home, or outside while walking or in a car, as well as professionally gave significant advantages over the dead-end technology of the minidisc. The advent of MP3 players in the early years of the new millennium displaced tape, CD, and minidiscs as media for listening to music, and consequently facilitated the incorporation of this technology into digital mobile phones. The capture of video as well as audio through these devices, and the ability to circulate material through the Internet, signals a significant transformation in the techno-aesthetic organisation of the black public sphere.

Schools are common sites for the development of the techniques and tactics of contemporary black-English culture. Residing within the structures of official learning, corridors are transformed into sites of freestyling, the backs of exercise books bear marks of identification inscribed in lyrical form, and playgrounds become centres for the performance of black art. Daz contrasts his listening to music in class on a walkman with a friend— 'one ear in my ear, one ear in his ear'—with MCing in corridors, in which walls were used as instruments in order to provide the beat through which their rapping was structured:

> Jungle emerged in the early 90s and it was like based on reggae dance-hall so we naturally got into that as well, and it was literally just MCing in the school corridors and just clashing. Some kids would play football, and we'd play football sometimes as well, and when we weren't playing football we was MCing in the school corridors with a dictaphone . . . recording it and playing it back.

Daz's sharing of a walkman somewhat modifies the privatisation that the device encourages, and his description of the clash emphasises the sociality of that cultural form:

> [It] don't always end in fights, it hardly ends in fights, it's just a friendly competition, just like some people play cards or they play dominoes, if you MC, or write lyrics, or you spit, competitiveness between you and your peers which results in you in a closed area, maybe beating on a wall or someone beat-boxing or someone playing a tape recorder and you battling.

The manner in which spatial confines are transformed into instruments through which competition is structured is an important consideration for the study of this art form. The role of the wall is replaced in the playground by the audience who form a circle around participants, urging them on and responding to their performances. It is worth noting how, through the simple act of beating on a wall, the 'context' is brought into the centre of the performance. Through this playful technique a grounded aesthetic is developed and structures the performance of the central actors.

The festive activity of these clashes is for all and produced by all. Afrikan Boy's recollection of the period in which he rapped at school provides a useful example through which to consider the carnivalesque aesthetic of London's black culture. He describes going with schoolmates to the town centre: 'Sometimes there would be a big group, there would be a big circle of like people . . . and you know, everyone would just start MCing or just like rapping. So its kind of like everyone would go in terms of spraying like a 16 or whatever. . . . everyone would go mad.' In the midst of the shopping and 'chilling' this black cultural circle would form, in which all participated. In contrast to Daz's description of rapping in the interstices of the school during 'break time,' Afrikan Boy refers to circles formed outside of his school, when he and his peers were free to be themselves. The verbal skills that are employed by these rappers facilitate the production of inclusive social relations. Through Daz's description of the language used in the school's interstices during informally organised break times, we can see how both the content and form of the carnival grotesque are reproduced through the city's black culture: 'Some MCs choose to talk about mums and family members and stuff. Some MCs choose to talk about the MC's lips and hair and eyebrows and *teeth*.' The emphasis on those parts of the face that either grow and are shed, or that devour and take into the body that which is exterior to it, underscores the grotesque humour of this play.

SYNTHESISER: IDENTITY FORMATION
IN THE BLACK PUBLIC SPHERE

The verbal skills employed in the circle of black-English culture are an expression of an essentially human quality. The expression of this quality takes form in the particular social and historical contexts of performance. The use of technology in London's black public sphere indicates a shift in the context and mode of expression from the primary orality described by Brathwaite to one of secondary orality. Ty recalls that 'the music chose me, I didn't choose the music,' and describes how his interest in hip-hop prompted him to explore ways of producing music. Through that process he was able to reproduce the feeling that music gave him: 'I started taping stuff and then . . . I got two tape decks and started trying to make beats or whatever, and I didn't even know what I was doing.' Through experimentation with technology Ty creatively worked out ways in which he could express himself. This process leads to the development of rappers' ability to understand themselves and their relationship to the environment they inhabit.

In a rather different context, Jeff Bacon describes starting to recite lyrics to rap songs as a nine-year-old in Northamptonshire, before he recognised that he could 'flip the record over and write [his] own stuff' at 15 or 16. Jeff's use of rap can be seen as a response to the monotony of village life: 'Northamptonshire is a very dull backward kind of place. Its got the highest crime rate in the country, above Brixton and Hackney—because it is that boring.' In contrast, Ty's musical exploration became a way of dealing with being an African boy in postcolonial London and the experience of social marginalisation: 'Being African was not a good look, socially, in London.' The desire and ability to use rhythm and rhyme are essential parts of the human condition. The experiences of these artists indicate some of the ways that rap facilitates engagement with the social and geographic environment in which we find ourselves.

Whether responding to socioeconomic marginalisation in the urban environment, or using thrilling stories of urban life in rap lyrics to cope with suburban monotony, young people, both black and white, are able to find common interests and develop ways of exploring who they are through this cultural form. Ty goes on to explain that 'the reason I say it chose me is because it jumped out and I found myself interested.' He describes the experience of developing his understanding of music as a means to explore his own interests and abilities in an 'environment that suggests I'm not special . . . "yeah, yeah, yeah. Really you're not."' By enabling young Londoners to find themselves, rap music produced in this city takes on the character of their interests, feelings, desires, identities, and the environment in which it is produced. Ty's experimentation with music-making without prior knowledge of how to accomplish this task is one of the ways through which he and other Londoners find and develop themselves through rap. The use of technology in the process of self-development also leads to a broadening awareness of the social world. The communicative technologies that enable participation in this cultural practice, at a geographical and temporal distance to performance events, radically alter the structure of the continuum in which Brathwaite found meaning to reside. The recording and distribution of rapping through these technologies significantly expands the interpretative community beyond the bounds of those present at the performance. It also modifies the relations between the members of that extended community.

Jeff's early involvement with rap music production differs from the experience of artists based in London. He recognised that he grew up 'in a bit of a vacuum' with regards to black culture, but his attraction to London-based rap gives an impression of the vitality of the rap music produced in that city during the 1980s and 1990s:

> I used to go into my little record store in Northampton, Spin A Disc, and they'd have Catch 22's *Tale of Two Cities* album, and there was a certain element of 'that's where I'm from' so I'm gonna check it out. But I was almost always disappointed to be honest. London Posse was the first time I really heard—saying that a lot of my early UK hip-hop exposure wasn't from London—but London Posse was one of like the first three groups I got into. And it was then that I knew that there was stuff there that sounded like me. Or that was from my shores that I could really get into and it didn't feel like a weaker version of something else.

The vitality of the sound of rap music produced in London is connected to the spirit of black culture in that city. As a result of his experience listening to hip-hop, Jeff eventually came to London to develop his artistic skills and ambition of a career in music. The passion that is produced within this sociocultural form possesses a vitality that attracts listeners throughout urban and suburban England. It is this aspect of black-English culture that lies at the creative heart of the social scene that attracted Jeff to rap music. 'It was when I was 13 that I then hit upon the idea of—oh right there was a whole scene and you can explore the scene . . . and you could dig into different levels of it and there were different kinds of it.' Whereas Jeff's isolation resulted in him mainly producing written lyrics, privately in his bedroom, his motivations to write were derived from the creative energy of an oral form.

Jeff's appropriation of rap may bear greater similarity to the form of subjectivity that Habermas identifies as the origin of the bourgeois public sphere, than the social continuum that Brathwaite and Johnson discuss. His 'privacy of appropriation' (Habermas 1989: 170) and distance from the sites of performance contrast with the collective production of Brathwaite's total expression. Jeff's emphasis on a 'poetic' style and his distaste for grime may be related to that privatised mode of appropriation. In contrast to the relatively isolated development that Jeff experienced, Ty recalled that 'it happened around me, and the next thing I knew I was fully engrossed in it.' In his own way, Jeff began developing himself through the exploration of a culture in which artists growing up in London were thoroughly immersed. It is important to distinguish the manner in which he began to participate in rap culture from those whose experiences within London's UK hip-hop and, later, its grime scene oriented them towards an intersubjective creativity. In explaining his self-development through a deepening involvement in rap, Jeff juxtaposes his educational achievements with home life:

> I'm one of those kids that was always good at English you know, and came top of my school in English and liked to write and that kind of thing, and I love word play—so I guess that was a big thing. And my parents were Mods and I think that's where my kind of Soul fixation comes from.

His teenage fascination with rap and the 'knowledge it gave' him extended his awareness of black-American culture: 'I went to Uni and did American studies . . . I ended up writing a dissertation about hip-hop and civil rights . . . and I already knew who Rosa Parks was, before I got to Uni, you know. And actually that's not something you really study in school.' Engagement with rap music did not simply influence the educational choices made by Jeff and other artists, such as Afrikan Boy. It broadened and deepened their understanding of the world and their own cultural development.

In an incident that highlights how the exchange of recorded material is used for further cultural production, Reain described how he brought a tape recording of a bedroom set into school:

> I remember one time—'cause this was when there was quite a few of us doing it—and we kind of split up into two small crews and we'd battle each other. And, I went home one weekend I think and I had a freestyle session with my brother and a couple of other bredrins. And we were basically just dissing the other man dem, and we recorded it on a tape, or whatever, TDK. And we brought it into school and we was like 'yeah we got this tape for you' and we played it like: 'right, what you got to say to that?' kind of thing. And then you know what a few people gathered round and was like 'well do it now' sort of thing. And like I went off on one, you know just rapping, I think it was in the corridor and

it was kinda—I was just on the spot just rapping whatever, just dissing man like—you get me [laughs]. Its pretty jokes still.

The role of humour in rap is an essential element of the festivity it brings about. Through the collaborative labours of different crews, the exchange of recordings, and the improvisation of lyrics, a special collectivity is brought into being in the interstices of the city and its institutions. An important element of London's black culture is reproduced through this social form. Absorption into black culture through rap inclines participants towards particular dispositions. In Seeker's recollection of working as a group to gain broader exposure, there is a suggestion of one way in which his awareness of the city itself was modified through his interest in rap:

It seems like once you start getting into something, whether it be poetry, whether it be drawing, all of a sudden the next thing you know, you start noticing and being attracted to certain elements of your field. So in writing I started noticing one or two posters for showcases. So, you know, we started entering showcases.

For his group, Any Thing Goes, performing as a crew was an important means through which to engage with the city's facilities, in order to broaden their social awareness and further their artistic development. Seeker's experience bore similarities to Ty's early experiments. He recalls 'finding means and methods of ways' to start recording their material: using a minidisc player as a compressor to produce a 'digital' sound, and then developing their material through 'the computer, using the bathroom as the booth' in order to further productive capacity. The collective work to build the studio highlights the collaborative skills developed through participation in the black public sphere.

In relation to his own artistic growth, Excalibah describes rapping along with artists before writing his own lyrics. He recalls deciding to transcribe Rakim's lyrics because he thought they were 'so amazing,' alongside being able to memorise whole songs. He and other members of his crew would compete to play the role of different members of the Wu Tang Clan in the performance of the complex interplay of that group's songs.

It was all of us. Just an equal feeling among us. We were all excited and would tune into Westwood every Saturday night, every Friday night. Like waiting in the house half an hour before the show starts. Got our little bag of weed ready to go, like 'come on Westwood, come on Westwood' and just like obsessed. We obsessed over hip-hop.

In addition to the collective listening that facilitated their remote participation in the black public sphere, collective performance was a key means through which these young Londoners developed. Excalibah also recalls listening to tapes at school that were being passed around just after he got into hip-hop, but prior to writing lyrics himself. The free exchange of music would later become an important indicator of the popularity of his own cultural production, and an impetus for the growth of the UK hip-hop scene. After performing at talent shows, Excalibah organised one himself, in order that he and his crew advance themselves. This was the beginning of his role in the organisation of the London hip-hop scene: 'We just wanted to perform, we thought we were the most incredible rappers, all our mates in school thought we were really good. So we done shows at Hackney Empire, Stratford East, Waltham Forest . . . Arts Centre. . . . I organised a talent show in Stratford East as well.' However, it was later, as a DJ on a pirate radio station, that Excalibah's organisational skills began to have a more substantial effect on the UK hip-hop scene:

> I heard tapes were getting passed around South London by a friend . . . I was aware that there was a little following for the show, by which time I was so into my UK hip-hop, like I was literally phoning everyone. As soon as a record came out I'd call the contact details on it and say 'right, let's get you on the show.' So I was getting Roots Manuva, Twang, Jehst, Taskforce. Just all the—entire scene—of that era passed through the Juice FM studio. . . . It was really fertile times, lots of artists around and it felt like a community as well. Deal Real records was the main spot for people to hang out at that time, then I suddenly had the idea of doing an open mic night there, which I called 'Live from the Legend.'

Transforming the record shop into a space for live performance provided an important structure through which to enable the flourishing of the UK hip-hop scene. The vibrancy of open mic sessions and performances by established artists inside Deal Real gave rise to spontaneous freestyling outside these events by others. Through the work of DJs like Excalibah, using material produced by MCs, the identities and interests of young Londoners were collectively organised through the UK hip-hop scene.

BUILDING A SCENE

The cultural resources used by subjects to fashion their social identities are also employed in the production of broader identifications. The practices exercised in bedroom sets, cyphers, clashes, and crews achieve fuller elaboration in the production of London's rap scenes. Gamma first developed his passion for grime and his admiration for MCs at his local youth club.[3] In the relatively informally organised environment of the youth club, artists and their audiences are free to explore their creativity:

> I started it when I was 16, 17. This was basically because I liked the hype when I would go to youth club and see everyone involved. I liked

the vibe, I liked the hype caused by the main person that was on the mic. And I felt like I wanted to be that person that caused that hype—one day.

(Gamma)

In addition to acquiring the linguistic skills of the rapper through practices learnt at youth clubs, the radio is an important mechanism through which familiarity with rap is developed. Pirate radio is a highly valued source for those who develop an interest in grime. Listeners become performers by rapping along to a favourite MC, recording radio sets, and writing lyrics to played-back instrumentals. When describing how they first began to produce lyrics, rappers frequently state that they simply started by writing about themselves: 'just talking about yourself really. About what you represent. As a kind of 14-year-old I'd hear what someone would say, like say their own bars, say I'm this MC, I'm from here, where I'm from is like this' (Klayze). Appropriating the forms and themes of other artists and differentiating one's self from them is one way in which social awareness and artistic technique are linked and improved. As a result of their shared interest and commitment, Klayze's crew, Red Hot, formed at his school. The crew constructed a position for itself within a vibrant scene in the school and beyond. Klayze continues:

Stryder went to my school, Tinchy Stryder went to my school. . . . Because he was so young but he was good he was kinda like a main attraction. And he was a really popular MC. So hearing things that he would write, then I would think 'OK, that's his style, he's talking about where he's from, his style. So I'm going to talk about where I'm from, my style.' And that sort of thing, and obviously you don't start off being the best MC, but you get better and you . . . your influences become stronger and you learn from your experiences and stuff. And you begin to write about what's really true to you, rather than what you've heard from someone else.

Klayze's analysis of other artists and his production of his own style and content foregrounds how participants in London's rap cultures acquire a distinctive *habitus*, through the production of 'objectively classifiable practices but also classifying operations that are no less objective and are themselves classifiable' (Bourdieu 1984: 169). It is in Klayze's identification of the value of quotidian detail in these circles that contemporary rap's grounded aesthetics and ethical affirmation of commonality are most manifest. His comments demonstrate how the activity within the circle produces a perceptive scheme that gives priority to the everyday, through the collective affirmation of shared experiences. In addition to developing artistic and social awareness, contemporary black cultural production requires the formal development of the process of composition. Alongside writing alone for later performance, Klayze wrote with his friend, Terror, from about the age of 13 or 14, prior to forming Red Hot:

> Me and Terror were always around each other, and was always writing bars together or about the same thing. Or we'd be doing like a back-to-back tune. So there was a lot of time where I'd just be at Terror's house or Terror would be at my house we'd play music in the background and just be writing bars to the music, to instrumentals and stuff . . .

By varying modes of composition, a broader range of formal features may be explored. The investigation of shared themes and interests becomes an important process in the shaping of children's friendships. A shared interest in MCing was a significant factor in some of the members of Red Hot becoming friends and, eventually, joining the crew.

The social relations produced through rap at this stage of development are not limited to small friendship groups. As described by Afrikan Boy, the circle has the characteristics of a larger collectivity. Klayze describes how the orientation towards producing tracks develops collaborative forms of working that enable both personal and social growth:

> It would be more about putting it onto a track. . . . When there was MCs around, there was DJs around, and there was producers around, it would be like 'oh can you make me a tune like this—with this kind of chorus, eight bar chorus, 16 verse, eight bar intro,' then they would work on that. Then you'd go to studio, then put it all together, then kind of send it around, like on MSN or give out CDs.

It is important to note how, in the grounded aesthetics of London's rap cultures, the process of consumption acts primarily to increase productive skills. The circulation of these cultural products was not directed towards economic accumulation, but social recognition and artistic development:

> In my school . . . there were certain people that would try MCing, but it wasn't really their thing. They'd go to producing or DJing, and see if that suited them more. And that's how there became more producers and DJs, . . . so there was enough for kind of MCs. I mean there was a time when there was just loads of MCs and no producers, so everyone had bars but no tunes to, like, spray their bars on. So there became more producers, more DJs, so it became more of a collaboration. For everyone there'd be like an MC who's got a DJ that they always work with. Whenever they go to a youth club they want that DJ, or they want a tune from that producer.

The growth of this practice in and outside of school brought about a division of labour. This did not only produce a particular form of cultural economy, through which crews and the wider scene throve. There was also an important ethical dimension to this economy, in which tracks were the means by which productive labour was given in exchange for social recognition of that labour. The use of digital technology to produce and transmit the tracks that were valued by Red Hot and the other crews in their field has been a key component in grime's popularity. It is worth emphasising that the practices developed within this scene were not primarily oriented towards economic accumulation. The widespread production and distribution of music for free facilitated a specific relation to culture, summed up in Gamma's peremptory statement: 'I don't buy music.' The mobilisation of digital networks for the expansion of this cultural economy develops an interpretative community of cultural practitioners rather than a market of consumers.

Following the establishment of a collective identity, Red Hot sought to publicise themselves: 'We went to youth clubs as a crew and we were always going around—make sure everyone knows the Red Hot name. We was always doing tunes in studio, writing bars together.' In a development from the establishment of personal identities as MCs, the crew worked together to publicise a collective identity and improve their collective skills. As was the case in the UK hip-hop scene, DJs have an important role in supporting MCs and organising the grime scene. In addition to participating in youth club performances, grime DJs have been influential in the expansion of the scene through digital technology.

Daz emphasised his relations with other artists through his work on pirate radio: 'We was around a lot of the MCs, all the major MCs that you talk about. I'm pretty proud to say we are part of that generation . . . Dizzee Rascal, Kano, Bizzle, all of them, Wiley, Skepta. We all came through at the same time.' Daz's advancement of his own role led him to further employ the Internet as a means of organising the black public sphere through virtual, as well as physical, space:

> We have two radio shows . . . we have a fortnightly podcast, which has 85,000 subscribers and is listened to on average by 25,000 people . . . that's about to transcend, or should I say develop into a video podcast . . . we put out a lot of mixtapes. We are UK mixtape royalty.

In addition to providing access to 'mixtapes' online, the release of DVD documentaries is part of a forceful pushing of the brand of Daz's crew and the wider rap music scene. Both Excalibah and Daz's work enabled them to construct positions from which their actions can have profound effects through the structure of London rap music scenes. Through their industry younger listeners are able to participate in the production of black culture, and established artists may utilise a variety of channels to communicate with their audiences.

In his description of the emergence of the grime scene, Dexplicit refers to 2 Step Garage, the development of crews, and aesthetic changes that produced a form of social organisation that foregrounds the local and particular:

> A lot of people say it starts in East London, in Bow to be precise. Like, I think towards the end of like the old school garage era, crews started to pop up. . . . So you had So Solid Crew, they came out first. Pay As You Go came out and Heartless were around for a while, but they too went in that category, as a crew thing. And you had others. . . . So yeah there was this sound that started coming round, it wasn't so much of a happier sound, it had a more darker side to it, and it seemed to be more based on MCs, opposed to you know traditional classic garage.[4]

It is worth briefly noting the Pay As You Go crew's use of mobile phone tariff jargon to refer to a mode of life in the city. This relation to mobile network operators 'freed' users from contracts and facilitated comparatively cheap communication. It also led to the practice of 'drop calling,' in which users, short of credit, would allow the phone of the person they wanted to contact to ring once and then hang up, in order to await the return call. This is suggestive of the technologically mediated relations between those in the black public sphere at the time of the emergence of grime.

Although Dexplicit acknowledges the geographic specificity of grime in the Bow area, he also highlights the influence of the South London–based So Solid Crew in the reworking of London's rap music tradition. Key points are associated with the movement away from the 'dancier' beat of 'classic' garage towards the 'darker' sound of 'MC-based' grime. By plotting the development of this scene through particular locations in South and East London, cultural producers, and aesthetic qualities, this interpretation of the field's history engages with the complexities of the scene's development. In contrast to this overview, Excalibah traces grime's historical predecessors, from the hosting of garage MCs, through jungle, back to Reggae sound systems. He identifies More Fire Crew, Wiley, Dizzee, and the 'Bow scene' as key actors in the emergence of grime, rather than So Solid Crew, which he describes as 'proto-grime.' Dexplicit discusses the attachment of the name 'grime' to the genre:

> At the time when all this ting was kicking off, when the dark music started really kicking off and everyone was getting on to it, the street term at the time—just anyway—was 'ah that's grimey, aah that sounds grimey.' It was just a word on the road that everyone was using. . . . Influential people started to go on radio and say it. . . . So if you say that on radio, or on Rewind magazine or something—like Rewind would call that grime, DJ EZ went on Kiss 100 and called it grime. These are influential things, and they're targeting regions, not just a couple of

people, they're targeting a lot of people at one time. So it just kind of got into everybody's consciousness and became grime.

Dexplicit identifies a convergence between the appreciative terms employed within the black public sphere with the activities of rap music producers and the broadcast media, in order to explain the way that various social forces came to cohere as a distinct scene. The combination of communicative technologies and a particular grounded aesthetic is of central importance to the organisation of social consciousness in London's post-hip-hop public sphere.

Dexplicit, who began to produce his early tracks at 15, states that 'grime blew up so much because it became so accessible due to music programmes like Fruityloops where anybody, a 13-year-old, could pick that up.' Pirate radio was also an invaluable part of the popularity of the genre, and he asserts that within a month urban youths could develop the skills to make grime tunes 'that could be getting played on radio, and you could hear your favourite MC spitting on it.' The links between friends that were involved in the scene with those who had access to pirate radio was an important element in the growth of the scene and popularity of the genre. However, grime's accessibility was further underscored in the characterisation of the track 'Pulse X' as a moment which transformed the consciousness and activity of those who became involved in the emergent scene:

> Rumours started coming around 'Pulse X was made on a Playstation' so everyone thought 'so I could make that tune as well!' Before you knew it everybody started making the same sort of beats. And that's when—I think Pulse X is the moment when the scene blew open and all of a sudden anyone could become a producer.[5]

Grime's aesthetic is related to the increased access to commercially available technology in contemporary London. However, before suggesting a link between the formal qualities of this genre and the exploration of the democratisation of technology, it is worth considering how access and expression are also limited within these arrangements.

Klayze's comments about sending files via MSN highlight the importance of broadband Internet communication in the contemporary grime scene. Social networking sites such as MySpace and Twitter, as well as online forums, also have an important role in organising the distribution of material within, and collective consciousness of, the scene. Wiley's posting of approximately 200 unreleased tracks on Grime Forum in July 2010 was reported in *The Guardian* newspaper as a result of tensions with the music industry:

> I just need people in England to listen to me. I need people to embrace me, otherwise I'm just in my own little world going mad. And people

who I want to hear me can't hear me. I've got all this music sitting on hard drives, and in the end it started to make me feel sick. I thought, let me give it away, and then move on to make the greatest music I've ever made. I just had to get this out from under me, then start again from scratch.

Wiley's distribution of almost 1.5 gigabytes of free music followed a tirade on Twitter directed at his management. The combination of access to advanced technology for storage, distribution, and communication with MCs and producers' productive skills does not readily fit within the record industry's commercial arrangements and release schedules. However, the creative talent cultivated within the black public sphere is able to organise itself in ways that meet other, human needs. In addition to satisfying his need for social recognition and providing an example of the ethics of free exchange, Wiley's actions reformulate the question 'what does it take to be heard?' for a new generation.

YOUR MUM! CONSTRUCTING A *HABITUS* THROUGH LONDON-BASED RAP

The antiphony and humour exercised through rap are significant sources of pleasure. This pleasure is connected to confronting the challenges of dwelling in postcolonial London. Reain's recollection of the 'jokes' derived from 'dissing man' emphasises the value derived from verbal duelling. Despite the competitiveness referred to by MCs and DJs in clashes, the vulgarity and insults appear directed to something other than beating one's opponents. Instead of responding to the recorded insults of Reain's crew directly, the other crew's demand that they 'do it now' highlights a prioritisation of spontaneity, verbal facility, and of bringing about a particular feeling through free language in the present. Afrikan Boy states, 'there wasn't really such a thing as who won. It's just like when it finished it finished, and then people would take away what they take away.' Nevertheless, judgements are made of the performances, indicated by the 'Oohs' and 'Aahs' of the crowd, and Klayze recalls the identification of particular qualities in MCs' boasts. Through the development of a free language by these incitements and judgements, that linguistic play contributes to the 'passion' that is developed within, and taken away from, the circle.

Bourdieu argues that a 'work of art has meaning and interest only for someone who possesses the cultural competence, that is, the code, into which it is encoded' (1984: 2). Here, the relevant cultural code is engaged through linguistic and bodily practice rather than abstract contemplation. Although Afrikan Boy states there is no such thing as a 'winner,' he does refer to 'destroying' others. The skills learned through this mode of cultural production are explicitly connected to self-making and unmaking.

The practices employed through clashes, or the Dozens, are means through which children begin to construct adult identities in their linguistic games. Through participation in black cultural production, young artists develop the means to challenge another's position, as well as to resist attacks upon themselves.

Roger Abrahams highlights the significance of these verbal contests in adolescence, when played amongst males. Although his analysis does not account for female participation in the Dozens, his argument that it allows boys to reject femininity and begin to develop adult, masculine identities (through insulting one another's mothers and allowing their own to be insulted) provides some valuable insight into this practice:

> By such a ritualizing of the exorcism procedure, the combatants are also beginning to build their own image of sexual superiority, for these rhymes and taunts not only free otherwise repressed aggressions against feminine values, but they also affirm their own masculine abilities. To say 'I fucked your mother' is not only to say that womanly weakness is ridiculous, but that the teller's virility has been exercised.
>
> (Abrahams 1993: 305)

Afrikan Boy identifies that there is something other than winning or losing that is taken away from the clashes he describes. I argue that linguistic skills, the ability to stand one's ground in the face of an 'attack,' and quick-wittedness are special stakes in this particular game. Importantly, the social solidarity produced through these staged 'clashes' is its ultimate goal.

Abrahams's discussion of 'talking broad' in the West Indies identifies how this practice affirms male groups, as well as events in which it brings the whole community together:

> This is almost certainly because it involves foolishness or nonsense behaviour which is regarded as a frontal assault on family values. Therefore it occurs on the street and at places where the men congregate apart from the women. As a rule, only on special occasions like Carnival or tea meeting is this type of performance carried on in front of women . . .
>
> (Abrahams 1972: 219)

At various moments, depending upon the position of an agent in the social space, the significance of the practice of a particular form of rapping will vary. Depending upon his trajectory, a rapper may be rejecting his position within a family structure, attempting to construct a particular social identity and occupy that position, affirming his position, consciously contributing to the production of a feeling of collective festivity, or a combination of these. It is through participation in this collectivity that the identity and identifications of young Londoners are structured: 'I called myself Afrikan Boy because—I don't know. I think people started calling me it. So it was just a name that kind of stuck.' In contrast to Reain, Afrikan Boy's name is a mark produced by and within that special collectivity and borne by him as a member of it. Klayze's analysis of other rappers' thematic and stylistic strategies, as well as Afrikan Boy's construction of his identity through participation within these collective performances, helps to illustrate how these practices are objectively internalised and produce black cultural identities. Through the everyday, necessary work required to deal with the urban conditions that are experienced by young Londoners from a variety of ethnic backgrounds, these social subjects develop cultural strategies that transform constraints into preferences. Attending schools and youth clubs in which rapping and playing rap music were ordinary, valued practices underscores the extent to which this cultural form is embedded in London's social fabric.

The visceral power of rap exerts a force on cultural initiates. They experience not only a feeling of sameness amongst others, but recognise rapping as a means of acquiring a social identity, outside of the family, and recognition for developing their innate human abilities in a way that is oriented towards reproducing that passion. Gamma's description of his absorption in the local grime music scene through attending youth clubs relates the music to a sense of belonging:

> Everyone's bubbling, everyone's kind of friends. So, like, the DJ would be playing the music and—obviously first of all I like grime music—and then all the lyrics and stuff that come with it. So you know, they have the microphone, they'd be saying their bars, and you know the crowd would be singing along and you know it gives you a real sense of belonging and you start to feel the music—*a lot*. And you know when the person on the microphone would be saying their bars if you like their bars you'd sing along, then the DJ wheels it up, its a nice feeling. Like everyone's shouting, making noises, and what not. That's the kind of feeling and environment that I liked and wanted to be a part of.

The antiphony at work in the scene that Gamma describes can be recognised as a profaned cultural inheritance from the black church (Davis 1985). Cornel West's (1992: 222) identification of rap as 'the African polyrhythms of the street' underscores the adaptation of the black cultural tradition to contemporary urban conditions. Away from London's youth clubs, immersion in the culture continues through working on and listening to recorded rap music. In describing his own absorption Daz recalls staying up to tape radio sets, falling asleep with his walkman on, and listening to the taped set the following day on the way to school and in class as part of a lifestyle in which he either listened to or produced music 'all day, every day.'

Connecting the values and feelings that underlie the name 'grime' and trying to describe a 'grimey feeling,' Gamma nods his head and gestures with his hand, fists clenched, attempting to communicate the ineffable through gesture. He states, 'there's a certain head movement and inside feeling—you just like—screw up your face and—when you're really feeling it you just think—"Yeah!"' In chapter four I will examine how the idiom of sex is used to explore the challenges of urban dwelling through this culture. However, it is worth noting Gamma's reference to the socialisation of subjective feelings and urges through collective responses to DJs and MCs' performances. Following Gilroy's (1994: 75) contention that we 'need to talk more, not less, about sex' may lead to interesting questions about the changing 'moral proximity' of the other in the black public sphere's contemporary structure. It is also worth noting that the motif of tension and release here may be connected with the production of subaltern subjectivities and the exploration of freedom.

Grime music production is geographically rooted in London, but the genre's naming and subsequent popularisation must be seen within the politics of the mainstreaming of black culture. The popularity of this form in cities such as Manchester, Leeds, Birmingham, and Wolverhampton can be seen as marking a later stage of development in grime's cultural production. In relation to this cultural politics, Klayze demonstrates not so much concern with a name, but rather a critical stance towards names and distinctions alongside an interest in playing with these distinctions in a forward-looking manner.

> KLAYZE: If you like that sound you wanna stick to that sound, but kinda switch it up sometimes. . . . I prefer over all producers, Hammer 'cause the way he does things is really different. It doesn't sound like grime, but it's grime tempo, and that's what I like. I mean it could sound like Soul, R&B, Electro-Funk, kind of everything but its at a grime tempo. Me, personally, I don't see genre like this is that and this is that. I kind of see 'yeah, this is good music' . . . Whatever is good music, for me, I kinda see like: 'I'd do something with that.'
>
> RB: Do you see yourself as a grime MC?
>
> KLAYZE: Yes, but only because I think that label's, that kind of title's, been forced on the scene.

There was a moment in which the grime aesthetic socialised the subjective feelings of a generation of working-class youths in London. However, Klayze's emphasis on going beneath the categories that distinguish music, in order to respond creatively to other artists, suggests a keen awareness of the politics of cultural production and an exploration of freedom in his own production. Even as grime's formal qualities change, and the genre loosens its connection with the time and places in which it took shape, the linguistic practice of rapping continues to address the conditions of urban dwelling and the subjective needs of its users and producers.

The importance of naming should neither be overlooked nor overstated in the development of urban subcultures. The names acquired by artists, crews, scenes, and musical genres are means through which the achievements of particular forms of cultural competence are marked. They also allow the forms of identification that are developed through distinctive modes of cultural labour to be made public. Young people also assume these identities in order to adopt a social position outside of the family. The significance of not having a name should also be given consideration. Artists' perception of the development of new genres, without names, being developed from within the grime scene can be linked to their understanding of the distinct challenges posed by the structure of the scene. This includes the place of girls within it. Alongside the significance of proto-genres, like 'RnG,' collectives without names (such as bedroom sets and cyphers) may be seen as part of a process of exploration. The construction and exploration of social identities and relations through these forms of consumption and production are an important part of coming to be an adult in contemporary London.

Much of the material worked upon by these cultural practitioners will be either developed for or processed within the circle of black culture. This circle lies at the heart of a network of social relations and processes. In the festive humour with which this circle is imbued, feelings of passion and sameness are organised in meaningful ways. Young people find themselves through this form. They recognise subjective urges and abilities in response to the music and verbal play, and develop them in order to more effectively deal with the social forces to which they are subject. The organisation of a *habitus* through rap also enables them to accommodate themselves to the positions they occupy in the city's wider structures. By drawing upon the everyday material they find around them, in written compositions and when 'talking from off the top of the head' in freestyle raps, the intersubjective relations produced through the circle are used to develop the innate qualities of its participants in ways that are appropriate to the conditions that they inhabit.

CONCLUSION

The appropriation of the black music tradition in London signifies the continued relevance of the cultural material from which contemporary rap scenes are formed. These resources include the forms through which the construction of an adult identity, outside of the family structure, is facilitated. They also enable intersubjective reciprocation through which social and self-understanding are acquired. Young people's adaptation of these resources to the demands of postcolonial London is an active process. Their constructive labours link them to one another and to a historical tradition. Through this cultural work they also craft deeply subjective relations to the spaces they inhabit and produce meaningful responses to their conditions of dwelling. These socioeconomic contexts can differ considerably. For some artists the crafting of lyrics may be integrated with their relation to mainstream institutions. It may even facilitate their advancement through the formal education system. For others, the music, lyrics, and movement within rap cultures may provide resources to sustain the pressures of a society that denies them the opportunity to affirm themselves within it. The enunciative position that rap cultures allow participants to occupy is a vital component in the construction of identity and the development of social awareness.

The use of technology in the appropriation of this cultural tradition facilitates the intersubjective reconstruction of the black public sphere in contemporary London. In addition to marking the aesthetic character of grime music, technology facilitates participative modes of democratic organisation in the city's rap scenes. However, the issue of access remains a central question within this public sphere. That issue is related to the value given to the circulation of music for free and how this shapes the character of these scenes. Importantly, digital technologies also contribute to the collaborative working within various forms of organisation that facilitate the construction of the interpretative communities in which these questions are discussed. The participation of friends, crews, and other forms of social organisation are fundamental to the reproduction of the city's rap cultures. Furthermore, the popularity of rap music production across the capital is an indication of the mainstreaming of black culture more broadly. The technological modes of its reproduction enable rap to weave its distinctive textures throughout the city. The following chapter will consider how its dissemination through mobile phones influences the character of London itself.

NOTES

1. Daz is not the actual name of this artist.
2. Seeker is not the actual name of this artist.
3. Gamma is not the actual name of this artist.
4. In order to maintain his/her anonymity the identity of this artist is not revealed.
5. In order to maintain his/her anonymity the identity of this artist is not revealed.

2 'On the Bus My Oyster Card Goes "Ding De Diing De Ding Ding"'

Transforming the Space of London's Public Transport

On an April evening's journey from Streatham to Tooting the actions of two teenagers prompted me to think about the sociality of public travel, when they responded to the anonymous voice that organises their journey on the 319 through this area of South London. After our imminent arrival at 'Tooting Bec Lido' was announced through the speakers in the ceiling, the girl closest to me mimicked these words, giving an almost exact repetition of this voice from her position at the back of the bus. Her friend, in turn, responded to this marking of the received pronunciation of 'Tooting Bec Lido' employed by the disembodied female voice, by repeating the word 'Lido' in her vernacular English, common to the area. By signifyin(g)[1] on this announcement the first girl drew attention to the incongruence between the way in which that voice is used to organise bus journeys and the girls' own understanding of their local area. Through the girls' use of repetition, an aspect of the cultural politics of bus travel was briefly made apparent. There was a conflict between their local vernacular and the universalising, standard English of the announcement. The final repetition (which isolated and corrected the anomalous word) performed a different function from the initial marking. The second girl asserted the primacy of their language and knowledge over that of the anonymous female's voice. Nothing further was said by either girl on this matter. There was no discussion of why 'Lido' was pronounced by the disembodied voice in that way, or of whether the announcement was useful to them at all; the job had been done. Their values had been asserted. Their common sense understanding of the world and use of language had been affirmed by one another. The incident makes apparent how the organisation of space on London's buses, far from being neutral, embodies particular forms, values, and relations, and makes these felt in the lived experience of passengers. That space is meaningful to passengers, who do not simply travel on the bus, but interpret it, communicate with one another through it, and perform social acts within it.

The bus is made up of a number of interpenetrating spaces. From its basic structure as a piece of complex machinery, a vehicle; through the safety notices and signs (inside and out) that mark it as a public vehicle; the interface through which the 'Countdown' technology updates bus stops with the arrival time of approaching buses; the 'Connect' technology that transmits live CCTV images from buses to a central location; to the various ways by which citizens are interpellated once they board the service; and the space that is used to advertise to consumers as the bus passes through the city. Each bus forms part of a network vital to the social and economic life of the city. The girls' signifyin(g) on the received pronunciation of the announcement reveals the social distance between this aspect of the bus's soundscape and the common cultures of some of its passengers. The use of these rhetorical strategies also demonstrates how that social distance exposes the official soundscape to strategies of diversion. Instead of taking place through direct confrontation, a sidelining of the bus's formal arrangements may be employed in order to assert the common values of its users. The soundscape of the bus is a synecdoche of the sounds of multicultural London. The form of the soundscape changes throughout the day in relation to the sounds of the wider metropolis. More flexible and cheaper than the underground and rail networks, buses play an important social function in maintaining contact between family members and friendship networks throughout the capital. This social function cannot be entirely separated from or opposed to the economic development of the city. Indeed, without a regular bus service some of London's most vulnerable residents would face worse employment prospects and greater marginalisation in a city marked by immense economic inequality and social divisions. By playing music on buses marginalised groups, particularly young people, draw attention to themselves, their values, and interests. They are also able to make these felt in a way that mere visibility cannot. In doing so, the space of the bus is transformed, and the dominant temporality is held in suspension. Deploying the advanced technologies incorporated into mobile phones, a set of relations are introduced by passengers into this space that are substantially different to those constructed through the received pronunciation of the disembodied voice.

THE SOCIAL AND POLITICAL CONTEXT
OF YOUNG BUS USERS

In the opening remarks of 'Way to Go,' the mayor's 'direction of travel' document, Boris Johnson states that his team's objective is 'simply to get Londoners from a to b as quickly, as safely, as conveniently, and as cheaply as possible' (GLA 2008a: 5). However, the consultation document adds a number of other aims related to improving the life and health of London's citizenry and to contributing to the production of a 'civilised city.' The mayor associates his idea of the civilised city with the collective participation in the city's governance by users of a variety of transport services. In spite of this, Johnson introduces tensions into the provision of a transport system that its users are happy with. His comments on bus 'ridership' place passenger comfort in opposition to the cost-effectiveness of bus services: 'It is no use having complete calm on the top deck of a bus, if that bus is itself beached in the traffic like an expiring whale. . . . Why is it that so many buses seem half-empty? Passengers may like it, but it is expensive in subsidy' (GLA 2008a: 20). Why the mayor sees a conflict between the economic efficiency of buses and the state of their social space is not made clear in this document. I argue that the production of a more convivial environment on buses may help, rather than hinder, the economic development of the city. A citizenry listening to one another, not with suspicion but genuine interest, is more likely to be capable of developing the cultural resources to deal with changing social and economic forces at work within the capital. Under the aim of improving the urban realm the mayor refers to 'an imperative that all road users have to think responsibly about the needs of each other' (GLA 2008a: 23–24). Although Johnson discusses this imperative in relation to road space, I suggest that the sharing of the bus's social space by music players, workers, and other passengers introduces greater opportunity to facilitate engagement with others' needs. Pursuing this opportunity may enable bus users to transform the mayor's uncomfortable notion of ridership into a substantive citizenship.

In the BBC radio four programme *On the Top Deck*, broadcast in 2009, the presenter, Ian Marchant, states that he spent time travelling around London on buses in order 'to discover what life is really like on the top deck.' The rationale given for the programme is the perceived increase in boisterous behaviour on buses in the three years following the introduction of free bus travel to under-16s. However, it begins with Marchant asking: 'What's the worst thing that ever happened to you on the top deck of a bus?' The programme does not make any serious attempt to develop a picture of what life is 'really' like on London's buses. Instead, it is composed of sensationalist flitting from youth violence, to the playing of music and loud conversation, back to violence and criminality. This is followed by a discussion of the surveillance mechanisms used on buses and a gesture towards highlighting the poor behaviour of some adults. Beginning the programme with a young person stating that the worst thing that has happened to her was 'having a knife held to [her] throat' and then seeking out 'the most dangerous bus in London' cannot further understanding of everyday social relations on buses. Instead it forms part of a process of demonising young people, sensationalising the practices of marginalised groups, and contributing to moral panics about urban youths. This chapter does not aim to discover what life is 'really' like on the top deck. However, it does aim to conduct a reasoned examination of the playing of music by children and young adults on London's buses, and the effects of this practice. Through this I also aim to investigate how black culture in general and rap music in particular contribute to the formation of adult social identities by young people in the capital. Going beyond sedentary notions of cultural production rooted to place, I explore how music can change the experience of moving through space. In response to Marchant's question 'do you ever think that people might not like listening to your music?,' he receives several answers: ' "Yeah, I think like that." "Some people sing along." "Everyone is different." ' That the playing of music on buses involves the consideration of other people's responses is made clear in these answers. I intend to explore the significance of playing music to the players and how it enables them to build meaningful relations with others in the city.

The pathologisation of adolescent behaviour not only contributes to the production of moral panic, but ignores important aspects of the modes through which people come to terms with their environment. The creative responses of young people to their world are not simply ignored but constructed as a threat to society, in a manner that is fundamentally self-contradictory. In his response to a petition regarding the playing of music on London's buses the previous mayor, Ken Livingstone, stated:

> Transport for London is developing a campaign to discourage all aspects of anti-social behaviour and crime on all types of public transport in London, and to further improve passengers' recognition of safety on the bus network. In response to concerns about the playing of music from mobile phones and MP3 players, the campaign will incorporate the issue of loud music, as well as smoking and drinking, and this will include posters in buses and at bus stops as well as across the Tube network.
>
> (GLA 2007a)

Livingstone later moved away from associating the playing of music with criminality, highlighting that 'when you look at the totality of the millions of journeys a day, the number of times there is a serious problem are very small indeed. It is very annoying that some people play very loud music, however it is not just a function of young people' (GLA 2007b). Neverthe-less, the London Assembly's Transport Committee restated this link between music-playing and criminality in 2008. Under the section of 'Making buses a safe environment,' in their 'Crime and disorder on London's buses' publication, the assembly members seamlessly move from reminding passengers of their responsibilities—'for example, not playing music too loudly'—to the need to deal with pick-pocketing and for 'raising passenger awareness of potential criminal activity' (GLA 2008b). The classification of playing music as antisocial behaviour ignores the fact that the playing of music on buses is an inherently social activity, and an important part of developing shared identifications and adult identities. Furthermore, the Greater London Authority (GLA) seems to suggest that collective isolation on public trans-port is a privileged mode of *social* behaviour. This stigmatisation of youth ignores the lack of sociability in public spaces. The GLA's association of music-playing with criminality indicates a serious lack of consideration of the everyday culture of London's young citizens.

It is important to engage with the marking of space by young people. Neither withdrawing free travel nor criminalising players facilitates a considerate environment or contributes to a civil society. Transport for London's (TfL) idea of London needs to be reformulated as a plurality, and alternatives to the suppression of young people's identifications need to be found. This may be achieved by challenging Johnson's suggestion that children and young adults are a threat to others and the Transport Committee's representation of music as antisocial or potentially criminal. Wakeford suggests that the bus ride can become a way of engaging with 'ideas of multicultural Britain, hybrid identities' and 'public space' (2003: 240). Through an extended consideration of how music transforms the social space of the bus, it may be possible to move beyond sensationalist depictions of young people towards an engagement with the forms of civil society that can be produced through public transport.

THE INTERNAL ORGANISATION OF THE BUS

During the course of this study TfL phased out the last of the old Routemaster buses. The loss of conductors on the replacement vehicles is one of the most significant changes in the social organisation of London's public bus service.[2] The working-class conductors were a human presence who would not only provide meaningful announcements, but could be questioned by passengers or engaged in sociable discussion. Although the removal of the conductor reduces operating costs, the anonymous voice further distances passengers from those responsible for the organisation of the service. Instead of drivers using their own voices to communicate with passengers, there has been a shift towards using the digitally stored voice to make announcements to them. This tends to impose a one-way relationship on passengers. Although safety considerations may underlie some aspects of this arrangement, it is open to challenge by passengers. Other aspects of the bus's soundscape reveal a more interactive relationship between its users and the driver.

Along with the departure of the conductor, the single bell has been replaced by a number of buzzes and beeps used as signals to both drivers and passengers. From the Oyster card reader's various tones, through the beep of the passenger bells, to the buzzing doors, the soundscape of the bus is filled with meaningful, electronically reproduced signals that organise this space, and through which the state of the bus can be understood. The integration of digital technology into the bus, which replaces the bell's mechanical sound, enables more comprehensive management of the bus through the soundscape. An irregular pattern of passenger bell, buzzing door, and beeping Oyster reader characterises journeys. This is accompanied by other sounds of human activity, including the turning of newspaper leaves, chatter, and the playing of music. The soundscape of the bus gives insight into the particularity of each journey, as well as into the general organisation of the bus. However, sound is but one of the aspects through which the form, function, and structure of the bus is produced, and a full analysis of how this space may be transformed through the soundscape should not entirely exclude the other aspects that provide the context of this transformation.

In addition to the various sounds that are now needed to organise the space of London's public transport, TfL uses posters and visual signs. In comparison with the London Underground, there is relatively little commercial advertising inside London's buses. However, it is worth noting that mobile phone adverts form the largest component of the commercial advertising inside the city's public buses. A number of signs advise passengers to act in a manner generally governed by a principle of safety. These vary from requests to not speak to the driver while the bus is moving, through prohibitions against standing on the upper deck or stairs, to instructions on how to escape the bus in an emergency. Further to these signs, which explicitly tell passengers how to conduct themselves in this space, the bus is also organised through the arrangement of its seats, handles, doors, and other fittings. The arrangement of the majority of seats facing forwards with large windows at the front and side may appear to be common sense. However, their configuration facilitates particular purposes and makes others less easy to accomplish. Certainly, by facing most passengers forward, bus users are oriented towards the onward journey rather than towards one another. This configuration of the majority of seats contrasts with the positioning of some (at the rear of the bottom and top decks) towards one another. The inward formal arrangement of that smaller grouping of seats facilitates eye contact, verbal discussion, and other forms of exchange between passengers.

The forward orientation of this space is reinforced by the announcements of the upcoming bus stop and the final destination. The successive announcements combine with the formal organisation of the seats in the construction of a linear temporality and spatiality, through which the bus's journey through the city comes to be understood. By contrast, the large side windows allow passengers to observe the bus's current locality. These windows also enable passengers to identify people on the pavement as the bus passes by. Occasionally exchanges take place between passengers and pedestrians. On other occasions a passenger may communicate his/her location or the location of pedestrians he/she has observed to another party via mobile phone, using references to local shops and landmarks. These occurrences highlight the network of relations that the bus passes through, and helps to reproduce, in the course of its passage. The ability to see out of the side windows does not necessarily conflict with the emphasis on the onward journey of the bus. Indeed, by allowing passengers to understand their position through various landmarks it can aid the framing of a forward orientation. By noting the different uses of features of this space I wish to draw attention to the subtly different social orientations that make it up. These are clearly influenced by the forward movement of the bus, but are distinct from the vehicle's physical motion. Both the forward and sideward orientations are beyond the confines of the bus; however, the insubordinate girls' activity mentioned above highlights that the internal space of the bus is also of importance to its passengers.

Further to safety notices, TfL's 'Together for London' campaign uses a number of posters on buses (as well as on the underground and the organisation's website) to ask public transport users to be considerate passengers. This request contrasts with the 'Trust Your Senses' poster, which appeals to the citizen through the sensorium, but does not refer to any responsibility for the use of reason. Significantly, the 'Trust Your Senses' poster asks bus users to immediately report to the police or staff 'anything suspicious' that they see or hear. Both the 'Trust Your Senses' and 'Together for London' posters invoke the idea of London as being in some way a product of individuals, either through the slogan '7 Million Londoners, 1 London,' or the notion that through 'a little thought from each of us' a big difference can be made 'for London.' The precise nature of the relation between 'Londoners' and the city is not made explicit, but there is a suggestion that London may be produced through collective effort. Nevertheless, by limiting the extent to which citizens should think about what their senses tell them, there is an implication that while a little thought may be required from passengers, they should only think a little. In particular, the anonymous voice's announcement that bus users should 'consider other passengers, and keep your music down' implies that there is only one resolution to the issue of playing music on public transport. This announcement supports one aspect of the poster campaign. The 'Together for London' campaign as a whole fails to encourage face-to-face discussion amongst passengers. Instead, dialogue is removed from public transport and moved to a virtual space—TfL's website—and the opportunity for collective decision-making denied. Although it is not made explicit, there appears to be an assumption that passengers are innately hostile to one another's interests and that public transport is not the space to work out modes of collective being. I wish to explore how, through playing music on buses, it may be possible to develop a more inclusive sense of substantive citizenship. In order to accomplish this it is necessary to understand how music transforms the bus through its soundscape.

MISFIRES, MISAPPLICATIONS, AND MISDIRECTIONS

The received pronunciation of the bus announcement is a prominent part of the structuring of public transport space. However, this voice occasionally dislocates itself from the function of constructing, not merely a dominant soundscape, but authoritative sonic events within that soundscape. Erroneous announcements, and the limitations of these preset sonic signs, are responded to in different ways. On several journeys I observed passengers ignoring the repeated announcement 'this bus terminates here' at successive stops. Passengers relied on their own common sense that the bus would continue its journey. Despite the announcements, they understood that they would be able to arrive at their intended destinations without the disruption to their journey heralded by the anonymous voice. In such cases the announcements became distractions in an otherwise properly organised journey. Similarly repeated announcements that 'the destination of this bus has changed' may have been ignored, but the following request to 'please listen for further announcements' places passengers in a slightly more awkward position. Unable to completely ignore the announcements, their continuation drew attention to the issue that the official soundscape of the bus (and the directions given through it) was so unreliable that it was necessary to ignore it.

Perhaps the most confusing error by the anonymous voice, that I observed, was that of the premature announcement of upcoming stops. On a southbound 59 an elderly man on the top deck commented that the voice was out of sync to the child that he was accompanying. Instead of announcing the next bus stop, the voice had become unsynchronised with the bus's present position and was announcing upcoming locations up to seven stops early. This resulted in confusion amongst some passengers. In addition to the difficulties this would have caused those unfamiliar with the route, the announcement was misdirecting all passengers.[3] The elderly man's comments, in a somewhat different manner to the two girls on the bottom deck of the 319, brought the status of the announcements into question. Errors such as these demonstrate that while sound can have an effective role in structuring the social space of the bus, the announcements themselves play a role in undermining the authoritativeness that is constructed through the anonymous female voice. However, in many of the cases in which I observed misfirings of the announcement, passengers did not seek an alternative source of information in one another. This indicates that they either employed their own knowledge of the bus route or they used other methods for obtaining the information they needed, such as looking out of the window. In either case this suggests that passengers would not have substantially benefited from error-free announcements. This in turn raises the question of the necessity of these announcements. More importantly, it also highlights their supplementary character. I argue that their form—standard English, anonymous female voice, repeating the present position, route number, and final destination—is considerably more important than its content in establishing a particular order. It is this supplementary character that gives the playing of music on buses its significance in the *détournement* (Lefebvre 1991), or diversion, of this space.

Alongside the errors made through the automated announcements, it is worthwhile considering the issue of their inflexibility. This issue is connected to passengers' needs to have basic information supplemented. That inflexibility demonstrates how the organisation of the bus service is ultimately reliant on human relations, and cannot be entirely automated. As I travelled on a 57 through Streatham, the controller radioed the bus, to turn it, because it was running late. However, the prerecorded message was insufficiently flexible, so when the driver announced that the bus will be terminating 'here' (outside Streatham Megabowl) his statement was immediately followed by a conflicting automated announcement, '57 to Clapham Park.' In addition to ignoring a part of the official soundscape, passengers did not find the more authoritative announcement by the driver to be adequate to their needs. Upon the bus journey terminating, they approached the driver in order to question him. He helpfully came out of his cab to explain that the bus was being turned around because it was late. Having found both that the driver's initial statement was insufficient and the automated announcement needed to be ignored, passengers took advantage of the opportunity created by the stoppage of the bus to question the driver about his statement. By seeking more information the passengers highlighted the necessity of ignoring selected portions of the soundscape and the fact that some of the sonic events that structure the space of the bus raise further questions. The conflicting announcement by the anonymous voice foregrounded the inflexibility of particular aspects of the dominant soundscape. This inflexibility is significant to understanding the space of the bus, and the strategies of *détournement* used to appropriate that space.

THE SOUNDSCAPE OF THE BUS

The irregular pattern of beeps, buzzes, and announcements that dominates the soundscape of the bus journey can be understood as part of the soundscape of the postindustrial city. Indeed, the dominant soundscape produced through the integration of advanced electronics into the bus never completely blocks out the sounds of London's streets: the traffic, road and building works, as well as other forms of urban activity. Throughout the journey the engine rumbles on, sometimes at a higher, sometimes a lower, pitch. Its drone is a reminder of the relation between the bus moving through the city and the other machinery that can be heard maintaining and developing the capital. In this essential part of London's social and economic infrastructure, passengers sit or stand mostly in silence. During peak hours the bus motors through the city fully laden, at its greatest cost-efficiency. At such times there may be a few, muted conversations between colleagues. The most significant change within the dominant soundscape, relating to this period, is the reduction in sounds associated with stoppages, when the bus becomes crowded with passengers pressed together. Following a high concentration of Oyster reader beeps, coupled with fewer sounds of the doors closing or of the passenger bell, over a relatively short time span, the bus drives past large numbers of stops on its way into or out of the main commercial centres. The pattern of Oyster reader, announcement, bell, and buzzing doors (with a lull in the engine noise) shifts to announcement after announcement, with the engine idling only at traffic lights.

This form of the dominant soundscape has similarities to that produced on a near empty bus during off-peak hours. The significant difference between the two forms is the duration of the engine's idling at transport hubs, and the lower number of Oyster reader beeps and passenger bells throughout the journey. This difference in the form of the soundscape marks the contrast between emphasis on the economic and social functions of the bus. Both of these soundscape forms (one produced by being at maximum, or over, capacity, the other produced by being near empty) generally share an absence of social activity. However, the soundscape is more likely to be disrupted, and become dominated by sounds produced by users independent of the bus's facilities, during periods of low ridership. Mobile phone users, for example, may speak louder when they share the space with fewer passengers. The disturbance of the dominant soundscape through mobile phone conversation introduces a partial connection with another location, through users' exchanges with absent interlocutors. Alternatively, others are made present through the silences in the speech of present parties. The bus is connected with other locations in a number of different ways: via the driver's radio, the countdown system on bus stops, and the timetable it is supposed to run to. Relations with other spaces are also constructed through sonic events produced by passengers, which often come to sonically dominate those sounds that structure the bus, the official soundscape oriented towards the function of getting 'passengers from a to b' (GLA 2008a).

THE *DÉTOURNEMENT* OF THE BUS SOUNDSCAPE

The connection made with other spaces through the playing of rap music out loud on buses is of a qualitatively different form to that produced through mobile phone conversations. The disruption of the official soundscape by music is far more comprehensive than conversation. The rhythms that structure rap music produce an alternative order to the irregular pattern of the official soundscape. This order is a digitally stored, asynchronous invocation of sonic events in another place; an ironic synecdoche of the soundscape of another space. Perhaps more significantly, the sounds of that other space now interrupt a soundscape associated with economic efficiency and the aims of the dominant social groups. The beeps and buzzes of the bus are subordinated to the sounds of pleasure, play, and celebration of the body. This interruption of the socially dominant soundscape functions on multiple levels. It is an assertion of a play ethic within this space and an aestheticisation of the bus. As a result of this effect, the playing of music also operates as a disruption of the antisociality constructed by commuters and facilitates an alternative set of relations to the social isolation adopted by disciplined workers on the city's public transport. However, there is a substantial difference between the sound produced through tiny mobile phone speakers and that produced in the dance scene.

In his description of a sound system being set up in the communal area of Stockwell Skateboard Park, Roots Manuva refers to a 'life-giving bass' coming from the system's immense speakers. He highlights the visceral power of music in his statement: 'It's just a bass thing, a volume thing. I don't know if I rose-tint the memories, but I remember it sounded so good, so rich. It's not like today when we go clubbing and it hurts' (Smith 2007). In contrast to the bass produced by such sound systems, the mobile phones used on buses have a pathetic insubstantiality. Nevertheless, the *détournement* of the bus space, through the ironic synecdoche of the dance reproduced through the mobile phone, introduces into public transport the potential of producing a radically new form of social being. In its disconnection from larger sources of power, volume, and bass, rap music gains the freedom of the city and the ability to introduce its temporality in a sphere far removed from that for which it may have been intended by any of its producers.

The reproduction of particular social relations through rap was observed on a southbound 59. During this journey I heard the lively conversation of a number of boys on their way from school. They sat in the rows towards the rear of the bus and, from my position in the middle of the top deck, their discussion dominated the soundscape for approximately half of the bus's journey. This discussion both ignored and competed with the automated voice as it intermittently announced the bus's route and position. The boys were bound for their own particular destinations, and the automated voice's repetition of the bus's terminus was apparently irrelevant to them. Their conversation was directed to themselves rather than to the linear journey constructed through this voice. Immediately before a track was played out loud, one of the boys rapped its lyrics. I was unable to see the rapper from my position, but whether or not it had been the same boy who both played and performed the song, there was contiguity between the two acts. Those actions took place within the framework of the boys' self-interested discussion. Although the purpose of these two specific acts was not to communicate information, they did not disturb the other forms of social activity the group engaged in. Indeed, these phatic acts were supplementary to the friendly discussion that the boys engaged in. They also bear some resemblance to the use of language employed by MCs to contribute to the atmosphere in nightclubs. Some minutes after this performance another sound file was played. A member of the group asked that it be sent to him next, following which a list of the active Bluetooth devices was read out. Shortly after this roll call the sound file was played again, presumably from the recipient's phone. The use of music and other sounds through mobile phones does not merely enable the act of sharing within already existing groups. Through the establishment of ad hoc technological networks, exchange between wider groups and individuals previously unknown to one another may also be facilitated.

Although the boys' conversation continued throughout their journey, their playing of rap music did not. A member of the group called out: 'You two, behave . . . there's an old man on the bus now.' Following this the music stopped. Then a short conversation took place between a man and the boy who had asked the others to consider their behaviour in the light of this man's presence. In this case, the self-regulation of the group did not involve coercion. However, in other instances where there is an attempt to stop the playing of music a different kind of social force is employed. A young, seventeen-year-old woman, in her description of an event in which she told a boy of about twelve years old to turn off his music, used hierarchies of age and size in her representation of the relations of power between them:

> 'Who do you think you are? You're sitting by yourself on the way to school. You're probably in year 7, and you're listening to these songs. It's early in the morning and these people are going into work. Have some respect and turn it off.' . . . And then he turned it down. Then I was like 'just turn it off or get off the bus.' And then he just turned it off and then sat there with his little head down. Still sitting there like he was a big man.

The young woman's justification of this form of coercion relies on rendering the boy, his interests and feelings, insignificant through age and size. Needless to say, this is not a strategy that can be easily employed in other situations. The relations of power in this exchange, and the threat of force underlying her ultimatum, are easily reversed. In a group discussion of A-Level students, which included a young man of approximately the same age as this woman, the right to play was again opposed to others' needs. In this case the young man stated that if he were told to turn his music off he would tell his challengers to go downstairs. Even though he was not concerned with appropriating the entire bus for one purpose (as was implicit in the woman's ultimatum) there was a greater force in his statement that if a passenger insisted that he turn down his music he would 'kick them downstairs,' than in the young woman's confrontation with the boy. However, both approaches fail the self-regulation of the group of boys above. In this failure they demonstrate their limited value in contributing to a more civilised city.

Whilst the force implicit in the young man's assertion of the right to play music *may* have been inconsistent with the sociocultural relations that his appropriation of space is purposive to, the woman's use of these relations of power in her assertion of the work ethic on the bus is a short-sighted and ineffective contribution to producing a socially integrated city. I stress the word 'may' here, as there was a quality of carnivalesque hyperbole in his statement. This quality contrasts with the seriousness in the woman's description of the exchange with the schoolboy. It is worthwhile considering the comic aspect of this young man's opposition to the imposition of seriousness on the bus in the light of Bakhtin's discussion of pregnant and regenerating death and gay abuses. In his discussion of the grotesque concept of the body, Bakhtin states that each 'abusive expression always contains in some topographical and bodily aspect the image of pregnant death' (1984: 352). The young man's words were accompanied by gestures which dramatised the act of kicking downstairs. His performance was responded to by the laughter of the other students in the room. This hyperbolic performance may be seen as his participation in a struggle against the 'fear of superior power.' In contrast to the Transport Committee's association of music-playing with criminality and antisocial behaviour, the laughter of his peers highlights how (even in the form of this young man's defence of music-playing and resistance to the imposition of seriousness and social isolation) his dramatised confrontation appeals to a sense of good humour:

> Ominously enough, each extinguished candle of the *moccoli* festival was accompanied by the cry of 'death to thee,' which had a joyous overtone. The gay abuses and curses and the mocking of cosmic forces had initially a cultic character, but they were later to play an essential role in the system of images reflecting the struggle against cosmic terror and every other kind of fear of superior powers.
>
> (Bakhtin 1984: 352)

Although the boys on the 59 had avoided any such confrontation, greater and not less engagement by adults with the values, relations, and identifications of London's junior citizens is necessary. Through such engagement we may more fully appreciate how their use of music and technology shapes experience, as well as how it develops their understanding of the city.

After arriving at the terminus of the 59's journey I took another bus northbound. On boarding the new bus I noticed rap music being played on the bottom deck. Instead of taking a position on the upper deck I remained downstairs. After a few moments I realised that the sound was coming from the driver's cabin. A number of different genres were played through his phone, including reggae and R&B. After a few stops I approached the driver and asked him about the rap song he had played. He informed me that it was Wu Tang Clan, and immediately asked if I wanted him to send it to me via Bluetooth. Bluetooth is a wireless networking standard for exchanging data over short distances that enables the creation of 'personal area networks' between fixed and mobile devices. Although I declined his offer, I was struck by this spontaneous willingness to share. The use of Bluetooth clearly facilitates this impulse, and promotes the development of particular forms of it. Furthermore, the technologies that enable a large number of sound files to be stored on portable devices and to be wirelessly transmitted are integrated with technology that allows those files to be played. This enables multiple modes of distribution. The sharing of music through mobile phones with strangers is a widespread practice. The young woman referred to above stated that she knew artists who relied on this method of dissemination to gain wider social recognition. The sharing of files via Bluetooth may be compared to sharing via the Internet, but these qualitatively different forms of network produce distinct social relations associated with the physical proximity of the participants.

In comparison with the bus driver's willingness to share, on a route 432 I observed two girls listening together to music through a mobile phone. After some time I asked who the performer in the recording was. One of the girls informed me that it was 'some boy called Specks.' She immediately added, 'it's deep, innit?' In contrast to the driver's demonstration of a willingness to share in response to my question, hers was to express her appreciation and address me as someone also able to appreciate this form of music. In both cases, there was a decreasing of the social distance between myself and the players, by the players. This did not remove all social barriers. The girls' response to my request to listen to the song had a cautious note to it. Instead of passing the phone to me or sending the file via Bluetooth, I was told that I would have 'to come here,' to the back of the bus. Instead of transmitting the file to me she asked me to change my position. This exchange narrowed the distance between us. As she held the phone to my ear the girls commented on the song as they listened to it once more, allowing me to contribute to their discussion from my position next to them at the back of the bus.

In addition to forming an essential role in an ethics of sharing, rap music plays a part in the production of a range of identifications. On a northbound 68 four girls sang and rapped to a selection of songs at the back of the bus. Their interaction with the music was somewhat more complex than that observed by the boy rapping on the 59 above. Instead of a single performer rapping the lyrics, each participant rapped a portion in interaction with the others. This produced a complex layering of sounds organised around the tracks playing through the mobile phone. Although this complex interaction did not continue throughout the entirety of their journey, it presented one form through which a set of social relations was reproduced. Their singing and rapping to genres from reggae to hip-hop, and artists from Beverly Craven to Marvin Gaye, was interlaced with self-interested discussion. The discussion, their singing, rapping, and the music that they used to facilitate these activities are part of the production of collective identifications. The use of transit space to enact these identifications was as significant as the activities they would have engaged in after alighting from the bus at Camberwell Green. Their after school activity was composed of the use of technology and the verbal facility they had developed through the use of music, which entailed the *détournement* of this space for their purposive performances. Along with the valorisation of the depth of Specks's music by the girl above, the interaction of these girls forms part of the production of a grounded aesthetics. There was no clear separation between art and life here—both were enriched and developed through the production of this complex performance. Their activities also brought into being a convivial culture, which is at odds with the fear, suspicion, and social disengagement expressed by Johnson and the Transport Committee, and fostered by TfL.

The grounded aesthetics that are practiced in this space embody an awareness that the structure and organisation of the bus is not fixed and uniform. It involves the enactment of cultural exchange and social transformation. In contrast to Boris Johnson's emphasis on getting passengers from 'a to b,' the playing of music draws attention to the human relations between those who travel through the city. These relations clearly involve the recognition and consideration of the needs of others. But this is not simply resolved by sacrificing music and play whenever they are confronted by other interests and social orientations. This recognition that public transport is a shared space, and that its use is negotiated, may sometimes be found within the production of the music itself and at others in the relation between players and nonplayers. The ethical dimension of this grounded aesthetic may yet be found to be a valuable resource for the production of an inclusive civil society.

THE DANCING BUS: MOVING BODIES THROUGH LONDON'S SPACE

Responses to the diversion of transit space through music are not limited to oral utterances, such as the appreciation of the 'depth' of Specks's lyrics. On a journey to Brixton I sat at the rear of a 196. A man played a selection of tunes from the middle of the near empty top deck. Upon the selection changing to a popular Bashment recording, a girl of about 14 orally and bodily responded to the playing of this music. She let out a tiny squeal and her body became poised. She then began to move her body subtly to the rhythm while repeatedly entwining and unravelling her hands. The older man, who played the music farther up the bus, was unaware of the effect of his actions. Through this sharing he had clearly given an unexpected pleasure to someone on the bus. The intricate hand gestures that had probably been practiced elsewhere were performed here, spontaneously, in response to the music. Significantly, the act of sharing that took place was not in response to a request, and its effect was all the more profound for being unexpected.

The social interaction that constituted the event was possible as a result of the participation in a convivial culture by two people that had previously not known one another, and who left the bus still unacquainted. The work that the two had engaged in to develop their cultural competence substantially changed the space of the bus. Though the girl had remained seated, the bus took on an aspect of the space in which this cultural form was practiced, whether that was for her, the youth club, or the bedroom. She had felt able to allow herself to use this public space for the pleasure that she gains through dance. Despite the impoverished sound that was generated through the elder man's mobile phone, the girl had the cultural resources at her disposal to make effective use of the transformed space. It may be that her willingness to allow herself to respond to music in this way owed something to her age. She had clearly not acquired the habit of private withdrawal (or discipline associated with the economic function of getting from 'a to b') that might have suppressed such actions. Her response to the appropriation of public transport space can be seen as a figure of a potential alternative to public disengagement and suppression of play ethics within public space.

The context in which this figure arose is considerably different to that in which I travelled from the area surrounding St Bonaventure's school, in East London, towards Prince Regent. Upon boarding the vehicle I observed that the lower deck was populated entirely by girls from another nearby school. There was a considerable amount of shouting and screaming on the bus, which was so overcrowded that it was impossible to attempt to see if there was any space on the upper deck. One stop after I had boarded, a number of boys joined the bus. Unable to move past the stairway, they remained towards the front of the vehicle. Some of the boys and girls recognised one another but, other than calls between them, the two groups generally remained separate. The boys stood towards the front of the bus, and the calls between the boys, as well as the calls between the two groups, now joined the girls' screaming and shouting amongst themselves. In spite of the noise on the bottom deck I noticed a small group of boys, just behind the driver's cabin. They were passing a mobile phone between themselves, MCing to the Giggs track that played on it. In comparison with the rest of the bus this group was calm and focussed. However, they were not completely separate from the activity of their peers, and one of their members moved freely between the rappers and the wider group of boys, shouting out to others as he changed position. This movement between the group and the rest of the bus reveals that, for these children, the production of this art form was very much part of their ordinary lives. Their self-interested performance was play without footlights, and a carnivalisation of this public transport space. In this case, rather than dominating the soundscape of the bus, the activity of rapping and playing rap music focussed the efforts of the group. These efforts were directed to reproducing social relations and a cultural form that they had acquired elsewhere. They now operated within a space which (because relatively unsupervised) was free for them to use as they found most appropriate. The activity of the other passengers on this bus was far more noisy and disordered than their purposive rapping.

SPRAYING SONIC GRAFFITI

The disruption of the dominant social relations through the bus soundscape results from maintaining, in transit, social practices developed in other locations. The reproduction of cultural forms, through dancing or rapping, within this space transforms it through the diminished aura that is produced through the play of these social relations. Even though the young girl's dance was not a response to rap music specifically, her actions nevertheless demonstrate the radical potential of music and technology to transform the space of the bus. However, that change was partial and, even with the combined efforts of the man and the girl, the *détournement* of the bus was incomplete. It did not appear that any other passengers were moved to respond to the music in a similar manner. The impoverished sound emitted through mobile phone speakers may invoke the practice of play and a structure of affective relations cultivated in other spaces and times, but it is insufficient to wholly transform the bus in the same way as the massive arrays of speakers that dominate the dance space in nightclubs around the capital. However, this part of an organic whole can be mobilised in a form of class, and generational, warfare. Escaping the scrutiny of the CCTV cameras, young working-class 'Londoners' call attention to themselves amongst city workers and other adults who might rather ignore their presence. Nevertheless, prior to being deployed in this role, the music must become meaningful to the agents that mobilise it.

In his work on graffiti in Chicago's ghettos, Herbert Kohl discusses the process of identification and the development of, and play with, identities that take place through this practice. He rejects the notion that graffitiing is reducible to 'the immediate pleasure of writing where one is not supposed to' and indicates that 'it may have to do with the important role names play in our lives and, in a larger sense, in the whole fabric of life in the society of men' (Kohl and Hinton 1972: 119). In comparison with the practice of writing names on walls, I argue that music becomes an important part of one's identity, and that the playing of music on buses is one way in which young people make public their identifications.

In most of my observations of the use of rap on buses, the music was employed in the reproduction of a set of special relations within established groups. The ambivalence of the hyperbolic statement that the young man above would kick those who tried to stop him playing music downstairs reveals the social conservatism at work in the appropriation of transit space through rap. The force of this utterance is directed at conserving certain social values, relations, and practices. The laughter that resulted from his dramatisation of this act manifests the humour that this force is attempting to preserve, in the face of threats of the imposition of seriousness and social isolation in this public space. His expression of defiance must be distinguished from the sensationalist images of violence in news programmes and documentaries, such as *On the Top Deck*. Furthermore, Boris Johnson's statement that 'adults are often too terrified by the swearing, staring in your facedness of the younger generation' (GLA 2008a: 9) does not contribute to an atmosphere of considered dialogue between passengers. Indeed, it even suggests that London's junior citizens should be hidden away rather than allowed to make themselves audible as inhabitants of this city. Clearly, the civic authorities need to provide a more considered response to how people, young and old, can live together and share public space.

Kohl argues that the 'way children choose to identify themselves to friends and enemies . . . or to associate themselves with groups of their peers is a crucial aspect of their growth. The way they and their friends stake out and defend the territory they inhabit is no less important' (Kohl and Hinton 1972: 115). Demands to stop playing music on buses may be interpreted as the suppression of something with which young people identify, or as challenges to their identities. The diminution and infantilisation of the school-boy above, through reference to size and age, reveals one of the ways in which these identifications may be dismissed. However, the lack of substantial engagement with young people's ordinary concerns by news media and the Greater London Authority is effectively *détourné* by the do-it-yourself publications of urban youths. They exercise their freedom to play their own and others' music. This is done principally for themselves, but they are nevertheless aware of the wider impact of their playing. The significance of these acts is not restricted to supplementing the reproduction of subaltern relations. It makes those social relations public in a way that mere physical presence cannot. Following Kohl's confession of embarrassment for spying on young people's secrets to one of his pupils, he receives the response: 'Mr. Kohl, they're no secrets—that's why we write them on walls. Only grownups don't read them' (Kohl and Hinton 1972: 113). By marking the bus through their audio devices, this space is transformed for purposes compatible with the values expressed through the music and the technology it is played on. As a form of publicity, the playing of rap through mobile phones also facilitates the formation of new identities and associations.

In contrast to the distance between the young dancer and older man, the events during a journey on board a 196 reveal the closer forms of association that may be produced through acts of making the space of the bus public through its soundscape. A young man with a dog, accompanied by a young woman, boarded the bus and proceeded to the rear of the top deck. Two young men already occupied positions at the back of the bus, one of who was playing rap music. After a short time the player struck up a conversation with the dog owner. When the newly formed group arrived at their destination they left together, continuing their conversation. In comparison with this, other young people recalled events in which conversations were initiated on the bus as a result of the playing of rap music: 'We went to go jam with him, to feel his music. We sort of made like, not a bond with him, but we started jamming with him; "ah yeah, where are you from, where are you going?"' The description of this exchange through musical and spatial terms foregrounds the form of the social transformation of the bus. There is a rejection of the term 'bond' for the relation produced and preference given to the more spontaneous and flexible notion of 'jamming' to understand the activity that took place at the back of this bus. Similar to the playing of the young female dancer and the older man, the socialisation of this space produced a bodily response to the music: 'One of my brethrens 2-stepped down the aisle to the tune.'

The playing of rap music facilitates the production of extemporaneous social forms. These are composed of a set of relations between the use of technology, dance and bodily performance, discussion and linguistic skill. Postindustrial time is suspended within this transformed space, and an alternative temporality introduced. The bus driver discussed above stated that he played music in order to relieve the boredom and monotony of his work. Referring to a holiday in Mexico, in which he experienced music being played out loud on buses, he valorised a more convivial organisation of public transport than that under which he was employed. The need to relieve boredom was also provided as justification for playing music out loud by young adults. Within the space of successive tracks, the dominant temporality of the bus's stops and starts is displaced. This initially disrupts the construction of a linear, postindustrial time within the bus. But through this the bus's space is invested with a sociality that brings the body, dialogue, and sharing into play. The references to holiday experiences and dancing down an aisle exemplify the extent to which an atmosphere of festivity can be created through the playing of music in this space.

THE PLAY ETHIC AT WORK

The assertion of a play ethic within the publicised space of the bus must not be taken lightly. It should be seen as part of the serious business of dealing with life in contemporary London. The cultural identifications and social relations reproduced through music are also at work in the production of an assertive, confident intersubjectivity amongst its users. This could be readily seen when, on a southbound 432, the driver turned off the bus's engine. This action was immediately discernible through the soundscape. No passengers on the upper deck responded, other than two girls who were playing music. Initially, their response simply focussed on the stoppage and its conflict with their own aims: 'I got places to go.' However, the desire to continue their journey quickly led them to investigate the delay in this public service. Alone amongst the passengers in managing the situation, one of the girls went downstairs. She seemed to have identified that the bus had been stopped because the lower deck was overcrowded and, as a result of this, she then told passengers to go upstairs. After announcing to the bus 'there are places upstairs,' the girls agreed between themselves that 'the driver can drive now.' One of the girls then informed the driver: 'now you can drive.' The driver promptly resumed the journey.

Interestingly, the genre of the music that they had continued to play throughout the incident changed from R&B to reggae, following their intervention into the management of the service. Although it is difficult to specify how this change may have been related to their actions, their confident assertion of the desire to get the bus moving ensured that other passengers did not experience a prolonged delay. The increase in volume and playing of sexually explicit lyrics may have formed a part of their recognition of their value, and that of their actions, within this space: 'My girl come up front and mek some gal gwan chat/She wet up herself when she see me Mavado rock.' The girls' manner throughout the incident revealed that their management of the bus took place within the relations of serious play they maintained throughout the journey. Their disrespectful reference to the driver—'tell the dick-head driver to drive'—formed part of their interpellation of him into their social world. Despite thanking him for resuming the service, they did not attempt to occupy the social position from which the official soundscape makes its announcements or adopt the style of its formal address. The playing of vulgar lyrics and the disrespectful reference to the driver underline the carnivalisation of the bus and the girls' challenge to the official order. Their reference to the driver's lower stratum draws attention to the overturning of the established order in the manner of the girls' efforts to get the bus moving.

In order to fully engage with the significance of transforming the bus's social space it is necessary to move beyond the consideration of the immediate role of buses in supporting London's social and economic life. Placing the bus in the context of the representation of the city itself may help to identify the potential significance of rap's transformation of the space of public transport. The contribution of the London Organising Committee of the Olympic Games to the closing ceremony of the 2008 Beijing Olympics incorporated a number of dancers performing various roles, dressed in business suits, construction wear, and casual clothing. Central to the eight-minute sequence was the London 2012 Olympic bus. After a human path was made for a child to board the bus, the top deck of the vehicle was transformed into a representation of the city's skyline. In the climax of this sequence, Leona Lewis emerged from the transformed bus. The R&B singer was joined in her performance by the guitarist Jimmy Page. The musical union between this black-British singer with the former member of Led Zeppelin presented a union of two strands of black popular music in the representation of contemporary London. How the playing of music on buses may have contributed to the development of this particular representation of London is beyond the scope of this study. However, some components of the image that this sequence represents may be useful in the consideration of a metropolitan imaginary, in spite of a number of problematic aspects in this attempt to represent the city.

The troubling elements in the representation of the capital include the exclusion of contemporary forms of popular music produced in the city and the idealisation of black-British femininity through perching Lewis on a pedestal high above the city-skyscape that Page stood on as he serenaded her. Nevertheless, the relation between the people and the city was foregrounded through the figure of the bus. The transformation of the bus in order to provide a platform for two generations of its citizens to play echoes the transformation of tens of thousands of journeys by ordinary people.

That the transformation of the bus for musical performance formed a central role in this representation of London to an international audience highlights the centrality of the bus to life in the city and the significance of the space of the bus in the metropolitan imaginary. It also draws attention to the extent to which black culture has been mainstreamed and its role in representing the city as a whole.

I want to contrast this staged and globalised representation of London with the rather more parochial figure of the young girl's spontaneous dance. The use of the musical bus as a representation of the city to the world contrasts with the negligent assumptions about young people's activities on public transport advanced by Boris Johnson and the Transport Committee. However, the choice of performers and genres produced an inorganic, calcified approximation of the vitality that the young girl's dancing embodies. Her response to the playing of the older man, who himself was unaware of the relationship his playing had produced, is suggestive of the fluidity of the forces that are embodied in London's black culture.

CONCLUSION: PUBLIC TRANSPORT AS DEMOCRATIC MOVEMENT

The economic cost-effectiveness of London's buses may have been increased by the removal of conductors, but the rigid, impersonal announcement is not an adequate replacement. Conductors gave a human form to the act of organising the bus, and enabled a dialogue that the announcement is incapable of and that drivers are discouraged from. However, the absence of the conductor, and the unreliability of the anonymous voice, has provided conditions for spontaneous forms of intersubjectivity to develop within this space. Although there may be conflicts between passengers' knowledge and the announcements made through the bus's sonic technologies, there is more frequently a dismissal, or refusal to recognise the authority, of the disembodied female voice. Whether it is in spite of or as a response to the inflexibility of the official soundscape and the arrangement of the bus's seats, the technology used by some passengers enables the production of a culture of exchange.

Through the use of this technology, new social relations may be established, music freely exchanged, aesthetic judgements shared, and the social body celebrated. It is necessary to work out ways of being together in the city that do not invoke the threat of violence. A civic culture needs to be developed that allows passengers to recognise each other's interests, without privileging categories such as age, employment status, or social position. The actions of children and young adults on public buses demonstrate that the primary purpose of playing music is not one of disruption (although this may sometimes operate as a secondary aim). The values embodied within these practices are those of sharing and the self-conscious cultivation of affirmative sociality. Both playing music and rapping to it form the basis of a shared set of identifications, values, relations, and needs. Through this, young men, women, and children make a claim upon public space and assert their right to be heard.

The GLA needs to engage more constructively with young people's public demonstrations of their place in the city. Instead of associating music with criminal activity, the mayor and the London Assembly should work towards fostering civic responsibility and open dialogue. I suggest that all passengers now share a collective responsibility for conducting the bus. TfL cannot rely exclusively on technical means of organising bus journeys. They should enable citizens to contribute towards making public transport a truly public space.

In addition to operating as an essential mechanism in London's social and economic life, the bus can be seen as a synecdoche of the capital itself. A stronger sense of shared public space and of being considerate may have an important role in developing greater social integration and collective understanding. Working towards these aims necessitates the recognition of the value of innovations made by young adults, both black and white, in metropolitan culture. Black culture has been used to represent London as a whole to the world. The stigmatisation of music, play, and sharing is a result of the lack of mutual interest and respect for others that is fostered by the GLA. This needs to be resisted, and responsible citizens need to hear the city's black cultural production and play an active role in enabling young adults to take up positions as valued participants in metropolitan life. By participating in the relations of mutual recognition and exchange that are introduced into public space by players, it may be possible to work towards a more civilised city.

NOTES

1. I use the concept of signifyin(g) to refer to a broad range of linguistic practices of 'encoding messages or meanings' and marking as a form of drawing attention to a third party's behaviour. In the present context the third person is the voice of the announcement (Claudia Mitchell-Kernan 1972: 315–316).
2. Since writing this chapter the New Routemaster bus entered service on a limited number of routes in London. The arrival of these buses in 2012 was accompanied by the introduction of customer assistants, restoring some aspects of the conductor's role to the city's public transport. In 2014 the New Routemaster operated on eight of the 700 London bus routes. http://www.tfl.gov.uk/info-for/media/press-releases/2014/july/route-8-and-38-now-served-by-new-routemaster-buses [Date Accessed 1 October 2014].
3. This misdirection is clearly a result of the 'misfiring' of the announcement (Austin 1976: 16). This misfiring reveals the way in which bus space is performativily constructed through the soundscape, as well as through its physical arrangements. Furthermore, the misfiring of the 'authoritative' announcement and the consequent result of this on that authority can be seen in inverse relation to the sustained 'misplaying' of music on the top deck of the bus by passengers and the social effects of these acts.

3 'I See the Glow in You'
Summoning the Aura in London's Post-Hip-Hop Culture

In his recollection of an evening at his old youth club, JJ describes a scene in which about 100 boys and girls gathered to hear the rapping of local MCs. The crowd, composed of slightly more boys than girls, counted about 10 MCs amongst its members. They had been drawn to the Tuesday evenings at the Forest Gate youth centre by word of mouth, spread throughout the borough. JJ recalls that at the centre of this gathering MCs stood around the DJ 'with the mic, in front of the decks so you can see what's going on and all that. And obviously it's important with sets that MCs have contact with the DJ.' The group of MCs 'spat' their lyrics while gathered in a semicircle—in concert with the DJ. Their audience surrounded them and contributed to the atmosphere through their support, but the MCs focussed on their own skills—'I'm gonna get tight with my bars, and get my flow tighter, and focus on the spitting and what I'm doing verbally'—rather than on the audience: 'It weren't like a performance type of environment.' The rapping (or 'spitting') was directed towards the improvement of their linguistic skills. The spatial arrangement of the DJ, MCs, and audience is closely linked to this sociocultural process. Their collective efforts made the night memorable to JJ because of the build-up of 'hype' as the assembled rappers passed the microphone to one another, practicing their lyrical delivery.

This scene represents a concrete event. However, it can also be seen to embody a set of ideal relations. The atmosphere was steadily built through the MCs' work upon their own artistic practice. This was done in contact with the DJ, and the audience who participated by singing along and urging them on. In *Music of the Common Tongue*, Christopher Small proposes the term 'musicking' to emphasise the activity of producing music over the notion of music as an object:

> Afro-American music making . . . has resulted, seemingly, in the production of innumerable music objects—and we have the records and the tapes and the sheet music that we can hold in our hands—but as we examine these objects we find that they are not as stable as we thought, but are mere stages in a process of creative evolution, caught for a moment on disc, tape, or paper.
>
> (Small 1987: 13)

In the event that JJ describes, rap existed as a 'text' only in so far as MCs had memorised previously written lyrics and offered these to audiences who came, through their familiarity with these events, to rap along with the MCs in the production of a social text. This is not a closed process, and MCs often change lyrics in light of the audience's response. Small (1987: 62–63) argues that a set of relations are established during the course of a musical performance and that the process of improvised musicking is negotiated. Although I will give a detailed consideration to rap lyrics in the following chapter, I want to emphasise that in this event priority was given to the process of rapping and the production of a particular feeling through the special arrangement of social relations. Following Small's argument that musicking brings about a set of ideal relations, I suggest that the evening JJ refers to was memorable because the combined efforts of the participants brought about what I want to term the aura of London's contemporary black culture.

In order to begin developing an analysis of this aura, I wish to discuss a further event: the launch party for Roll Deep's album *The Return of the Big Money Sound*. Following the performance of a song early in their set, the crew made an appeal to the audience: 'Make some noise. Come on we need more energy than that, please.' This was followed by directions to the engineer to alter the sound and light levels—'the music needs to be louder out there and there's a big bright light that's shining in my face. I can't work with it.' As the night continued, the technical adjustments to the auditory and visual environment combined with the efforts of the MCs and audience to generate the atmosphere of the event. The technical, linguistic, and participatory work resulted in energetic dancing and cheering in response to the performance.

I want to briefly pause to consider the appeal to the audience and engineer, along with the performance that preceded it. These make apparent some of the constituent elements of the aura that rapping contributes to bringing about. The use of amplified sound and lighting arrangements, with the audience in relative darkness, combined with the linguistic and physical efforts of the performers and audience to bring about the process that the MC's appeal for 'more energy' was directed to. The chorus of the song performed prior to that appeal involved the lead MC rapping, 'If I eat, I eat with my crew/ If I smoke weed, smoke weed with my crew . . .' as the rest of the crew emphasised the last few words of each bar. Both the lyrical content of the song and the structure of the performance emphasise the relationship between the members of the crew. The appeal to the audience foregrounds the relationship between the members of the crew and of the audience as constitutive of a larger whole. That greater whole does not precede the performance. It is produced through the combined efforts of participants. In addition to representing a development from the youth club scene, I want to use this particular performance as an example through which to identify the different investments that participants have in this cultural form. The MCs work together as a crew in order to promote their album and to invigorate the audience, who have paid to be present at the event but who also have something more to give. Together, they all must exert an effort to produce the aura of this event.

THE AURA OF THE ARTWORK IN THE AGE
OF DIGITAL PRODUCTION

The aura, produced in spaces such as these, is brought about through a process that involves various forms of investments: economic, cultural, and social. Although the economic aspects of the aura may be considered in relation to Roll Deep's event (including its role in the launch of their album, the money charged for entry to the performance, and the payment of Afrikan Boy to perform as the opening act), I will leave consideration of the aura's connection to rap artists' commercial activities to chapter five. I wish to use this space to address the sociocultural organisation of rappers' work. It is through the productive relations between artists, audience members, and the artwork that the aura is activated. In 'The Work of Art in the Age of Mechanical Reproduction,' Walter Benjamin considered the development of art over the course of Western civilisation, up to the effect of film in transforming the artists and audiences' relation to the artwork in his time. For Benjamin, the aura was inseparable from the unique existence of the work of art in time and space: 'We define the aura as the unique phenomenon of distance, however close it may be' (2007: 222). As a result of the technical processes of mechanical reproduction this quality has depreciated:

> One might subsume the eliminated element in the term 'aura' and go on to say: that which withers in the age of mechanical reproduction is the aura of the work of art. This is a symptomatic process whose significance points beyond the realm of art. One might generalize by saying: the technique of reproduction detaches the reproduced object from the domain of tradition.
>
> (Benjamin 2007: 223–224)

Benjamin argued that, as a result of the detachment of the artwork from its ritual function and the reduced distance between the audience and the work, the function of art has come to be based on political practice. Through the use of this concept I want to examine the manner in which MCs and DJs organise their audiences' collective consciousness. By attending to the processual character of the artwork in the context of digital production in London's black public sphere, I want to emphasise the embodied, corporeal quality of the aura. Benjamin drew on Pirandello's discussion of film to highlight the changed position of the film actor in relation to that of the stage actor:

> 'The film actor' wrote Pirandello 'feels as if in exile—exiled not only from the stage but also from himself. With a vague sense of discomfort

he feels inexplicable emptiness: his body loses its corporeality, it evapo-rates, it is deprived of reality. . . .' This situation might also be character-ised as follows: for the first time . . . man has to operate with his whole living person, yet forgoing its aura.

(Benjamin 2007: 229)

The work undertaken by MCs and DJs attempts to reinvest the collective body with its unique aura. However, the relationship that they establish with their public is not one of contemplative immersion, but of tactile absorp-tion. Benjamin's discussion of architecture is relevant here:

Buildings are appropriated in a twofold manner: by use and by perception—or rather, by touch and sight. Such appropriation cannot be understood in terms of the attentive concentration of a tourist before a famous building. On the tactile side there is no counterpart to contemplation on the optical side. Tactile appropriation is accomplished not so much by attention as by habit.

(Benjamin 2007: 240)

By employing Benjamin's conception of the aura I want to draw attention to the manner in which audiences appropriate rap music through tactile apperception, as well as how MCs and DJs offer their work to their public.

The MCs' rapping organises the audiences' interpretative work. Their lyrics urge dancers to explore the potentiality of the soundscape in which they are immersed and bring the audience together as an interpretative com-munity. My discussion of the aura aims to engage with a variety of embod-ied identifications with MCs' performative utterances. Bourdieu's discussion of the body as a materialisation of class taste may be helpful in understand-ing the dance space as a site for the expression of a range of values:

It follows that the body is the most indisputable materialization of class taste, which manifests in several ways, . . . its visible form, which express in countless ways a whole relation to the body, i.e., a way of treating it, . . . maintaining it, which reveals the deepest disposition of the habitus.

(Bourdieu 1984: 190)

Whereas my earlier discussion of grounded aesthetics focussed on the role of verbal play in producing forms of social exploration and collectivity, I wish to shift focus in the present chapter, to examine how MCs' linguistic utter-ances are registered in the body. On the dance floor MCs' audiences explore feelings and urges related to their conditions of dwelling that may have not yet achieved fully conscious expression. Through bodily gesture and verbal repetition of rap lyrics, audience members produce identification with MCs' linguistic utterances. Bourdieu's discussion of popular art foregrounds how

verbal play is mobilised in the construction of oppositional identities. He
states:

> It is no accident that the only area of working-class practice in which style
> itself achieves stylization is that of language, with argot, the language of
> leaders, 'godfathers,' which implicitly affirms a counter-legitimacy with,
> for example, the intention of deriding or desacralizing the 'values' of the
> dominant morality and aesthetic.
>
> (Bourdieu 1984: 395)

The linguistic skills employed in exploring experiences of freedom and collectivity in the crew, cypher, and circle also function in the production of
identification and identity through corporeal appropriation.

Before turning to a concrete example of an embodied response to rap
lyrics, Austin's consideration of the speech act and Voloshinov's discussion
of the linguistic relation between the psyche and ideology are relevant to the
analysis of how a collective consciousness is organised through rap music
events. Voloshinov's concern with the task of objectively defining the psyche
led him to emphasise the socio-ideological nature of the individual psyche:

> A rigorous distinction must always be made between the concept of
> the individual as a natural specimen without reference to the social
> world (i.e., the individual as object of the biologist's knowledge and
> study) and the concept of individuality which has the status of an
> ideological-semiotic superstructure over the natural individual and
> which, therefore, is a social concept.
>
> (Voloshinov 1973: 34)

The psyche is shaped not only by biological factors but also by social conditions. Voloshinov goes on to argue that the sign is 'common territory'
for both the psyche (the social individual) and the socio-ideological world
through which the psyche is constructed: 'Between the psyche and ideology no boundaries do or can exist from the point of view of ideological
content itself.' Nevertheless, the inner sign (or inner experience) must be
understood within the context of a particular psyche, whereas the outer sign
has achieved fuller distinction and differentiation as a result of its ideological expression:

> Any cognitive thought . . . comes into existence . . . with an orientation
> toward an ideological system of knowledge where that thought will find
> its place. My thought, in this sense, from the very start belongs to an
> ideological system and is governed by its set of laws. But, at the same
> time, it belongs to another system that is just as much a unity and just
> as much in possession of its own set of laws—the system of my psyche.
> The unity of this second system is determined not only by the unity of

my biological organism but also the whole aggregate of conditions of
life and society in which that organism has been set.

(Voloshinov 1973: 35)

This distinction allows us to examine how subjective urges are socialised
within the black public sphere. In the context of the nightclub or concert,
MCs invite their audiences to give expression to their subjective urges.

> The more closely the inner sign is interwoven with the unity of this psy-
> chic system and the more strongly marked by biological and biographic
> factors, the further away will the inner sign be from fully fledged ideo-
> logical expression. Conversely, as it approaches closer to its ideological
> formulation and embodiment, the inner sign may be said to cast off the
> bonds of the psychic context in which it had been held.

Bodily responses to MCs' lyrics highlight the social force of these linguistic
utterances. It is through the force of the rapper's speech acts that dancers' bodies give expression to their inner experience and produce social identification.

J.L. Austin's distinction between illocution and perlocution is relevant to
the collective production of the aura. In his discussion of speech acts Austin states that we 'perform *illocutionary acts* such as informing, ordering,
warning, undertaking, &c., i.e. which have a certain (conventional) force'
and that 'we may also perform *perlocutionary acts*: what we bring about
or achieve by saying something' (1976: 108). While the MC and DJ occupy
privileged positions in nightclubs and concert events, the audience plays a
crucial role in bringing about the collective experience in these spaces. Austin's statement that '[s]aying something will often, or even normally, produce
certain consequential effects upon the feelings, thoughts or actions of the
audience, or the speaker' (1976: 101) is useful in consideration of the antiphony that structures the collective performances of the DJ, MC, and audience.
The range of audience members' responses to the artists' performances constitutes the total expression of this interpretative community. This enables
the exploration of subjective experience and the production of social identification. It is in the total expression of the perlocutionary act that the aura
is constituted. The social force of the MC's utterance is an important consideration here, and must be seen as a product of the relation that the MC
negotiates with the other members of the assembled gathering. Through the
collective production of the aura, participants explore the meaning of MCs'
lyrics in a manner that is not limited to their sense and reference.

THE AURA OF LONDON'S CONTEMPORARY RAP CULTURE

The active role played by audience members in the production of the aura
can be seen through 19-year-old Peter's description of the feeling he gains

from grime music: 'You've got power and you can do anything you want.'[1] His use of grime to experience feelings of empowerment is directly connected to its being played communally. Prioritising physical response over disinterested contemplation, he insists: 'Personally, I think it would be a waste to listen to the music playing and just sit down, and listen to it—doing nothing.' In clarification of what he does with the 'power' that he feels the music gives him, Peter states: 'I'll spit the lyrics to it as well, in the same *tone* as the actual artist does it as well. For example, Lethal B, he makes these noises. I'll make the same noise as well, because it gives off the same feeling' (Peter's emphasis). In contexts such as youth- and nightclubs, sonic technology is used to facilitate a process rather than to produce a product. Peter's adoption of an enunciative position draws attention to the narrowing of the gap between audience and artist, and the production of a social continuum, through this total expression.

Peter's emphasis on tone above the semantic content of lyrics in his use of the freedom granted through music is significant. It may aid the analysis of how the aesthetic experiences produced through rapping are responded to through the body. Following his statement that 'the music permits you to do what the hell you want,' I argue that the phatic element of the MCs' rapping conveys a freedom to use the music to explore the feelings that it produces within the audience. This phatic element may be overlooked in textual analysis, but forms an important part of rap's social value. Rap, through its social function, empowers audience members to explore their collective energy and animates the dance floor as a whole.

Describing the subjective experience produced in response to the lyrics of Lethal B's 'Pow!,' on the 'Forward Riddim' instrumental, Peter states: 'It kind of feels like you're telling someone off and it feels good at the same time. I can't really describe it.' This reference to disciplining another may be linked to Peter's emergence into adulthood. The reversal of social relations, in which he adopts the position of the adult while using another club goer to perform the act of being disciplined upon, is also connected by him to the ineffable. His professed inability to fully describe the feeling that he has already—at least in part—related suggests that the urges that the music allows him to explore are deeply felt. Rapping and gesturing with others, in the social freedom produced by the musicking, forms part of the working through of deeply felt emotions. It is significant that Peter emphasises noises and tone in his discussion of his response to grime tracks. In doing so he draws attention to how the material dimension of music and language are employed in the exploration of feelings that have not yet achieved full ideological expression.

The lyrics offered to the audience by the MC or DJ are incorporated into the psyche of audience members through a process of reorientation to their given context. The collective response to the lyrics through common gestures and verbal expression also highlight the ritualisation of this process in order to explore common concerns. The lyrics are employed in the construction of a meaningful relation between the subjective and communal. For Peter, the music allows him to express deeply felt feelings in a socially acceptable manner. His assertion that 'whenever that [track 'Pow!'] comes on in any club everyone will just go mad' suggests that the ability to express his feelings amongst others produces a commonality, a collective talking in tongues. In his explanation of what he means by 'go mad,' he emphasises purposive collective performance: 'Well, they'll just you know. Everyone will be spitting the lyrics in the same tone as he does, they'll be making gestures as well—like the gun gesture. But in some cases it does get really violent. This is why I'm picky with my clubs.' Peter's admission of the possibility of violence that may result from what he describes as 'pretend' confrontations attempts to negotiate the boundary between expressing urges in a sociably acceptable manner and the possibility that ritualised gesture may lead to physical violence. His position on the boundaries of 'violence' and ritualised release in nightclubs is significant, and I will consider this issue later in this chapter. However, before dealing with that matter in detail, it is necessary to examine how the collective expression of feelings takes place through physical gesture, as well as verbal enunciation. There is an affirmation of rap's relation to the body in this collective response. It is also necessary to briefly consider the position of this collective affirmation of black culture in the wider context of postcolonial London and the securitocracy that orders daily life in the capital.

696: THAT'S THE SOUND OF THE BEAST

The limited number of major grime events held in London was related, by artists and club goers, to the policing of the city's entertainment. In particular '696,' or the 'Promotion Risk Assessment Form—696,' was identified as a key instrument in suppressing the scene's growth in the capital. The original form asked promoters for the 'make-up' of the target audience. The use of this question was abandoned by the metropolitan police, following objections by artists and a review by the London Assembly's Metropolitan Police Association. Although Detective Chief Superintendent Richard Martin claimed that the police 'dropped the question about which type of music will be played [because] it really does not add anything' (Guardian 2009), the MPA's report reasoned that this and a number of other questions in the 696 form had the 'potential to be perceived as racially discriminatory.'[2] The questions to which the MPA referred included the request for details about the 'make-up' of those attending music events and details of the music to be played. Several interviewees highlighted that the policing of music in the capital disproportionately affected black artists, and one claimed that some rap artists could not perform in London at all.

All the events that I attended in London during the course of this study would have been subject to the metropolitan police force's regime of risk assessment. This raises wider questions about the political economy of London's nightlife than I am able to deal with here. These include issues of who may perform, the influence that the police have over what may be played, and the types of venues that are accessible to black performers. During the course of this study, a central London club that had hosted a number of grime events closed down. The future of another club, Plastic People, was put into doubt after the police served notice that they wanted the club's licence to be reviewed in order to prevent 'public nuisance' and 'crime and disorder.' During the same period, Matter, a club on the Greenwich peninsular, began to host grime events. Its location contrasted with the busy London streets leading to Plastic People. The wide-open space that allowed large numbers of officers to assemble and observe club goers on their way to the venue may have posed fewer challenges to the policing of the area.

These developments signify a very different political economy to the sound systems and Blues parties of London's black culture in which Bovell and Johnson participated. Furthermore, although some of the bouncers at the events I attended behaved in a civil manner, the use of metal barriers and metal detectors and the scanning of identity cards materialised a sense of the city's securitocracy. However, the effect of the militarisation of civilian life was heightened on a number of occasions at the Ministry of Sound and other clubs when bouncers barked orders at me and other club goers or were unnecessarily aggressive in their manner of organising our entry into the venue. One of the events that I discuss in the following sections took place outside London. By highlighting the regulatory context that may have forced that event to be held in Bristol rather than London, I want to highlight the political significance of practices within the event itself.

TIME, SPACE, AND . . . THE 'ROLEX SWEEP'

Peter's description of dancing to grime music emphasises the commonality of responses to the music. Live rapping over recorded tracks also works toward the individuation of responses to the soundscape that the audience is immersed in. At an event in the Ministry of Sound nightclub, in South London, the MC called to the audience over a Tribal House track: 'Whose got a futuristic skank inside the place? I wanna see some funky skank. Yeah man, we're taking you deep down inside the bush right now.' His MCing employed themes of temporality and spatiality, urging dancers to explore futurity through the music while locating a spatiality 'deep down inside the bush' in a process of exploring human possibilities. The live MCing enabled a more dialogical relation to the soundscape than the events described by Peter. In addition to allowing the DJ to adapt her selection of tracks to the audience, the MC's rapping was directed to developing particular ideas in relation to those selections.

Later in the event, these themes were further explored through Skepta's track 'Rolex Sweep.' The MC followed the track's request that its audience 'count with me' by asking, 'who can do the Rolex Sweep?' Interweaving his raps with those on the track, he urged the audience to produce 'futuristic skanks.' Although a large number of dancers responded to his call, he singled out two young men. Their performances incorporated elements of the dance featured in the song's music video, with gestures of their own. They swept their arms in a circle while rocking their bodies back and forth, with heads held high. The relation between the MC's rapping, the music played by the DJ, and the audience's dancing was oriented to bringing various cultural resources together to be worked upon in the space of the dance. The live MCing and the 'Rolex Sweep' track combined commercial branding, temporality, spatiality, and movement. These concepts were offered to the audience through the soundscape. The exaggerated gestures of the dancers singled out by the MC were the mode through which they participated in the aura, *the process of working upon the resources,* of London's rap culture. The MC's rapping organised the dancers' exploration of the potentiality of the DJ's musicking. His occasional calls to the audience (such as 'oli, oli, oli') maintained contact with the audience as a whole and developed their active participation (when they respond 'oi, oi, oi') in the unfolding of the event.

The antiphonic calls of this MC worked in a similar manner to the insertion of stock rhymes and the use of repeated phrases by other artists, including Wiley and Scratchy. They bring the audience into the wider performance. Through these linguistic strategies the crowd is able to respond and collectively adopt an enunciative position in relation to the MC's rapping. The boundaries of the performance are expanded to include the audience as active participants. Susan Stewart's discussion in *Nonsense* is relevant here:

> Play is an intrinsically rewarding activity. It is done 'for play's sake.' It takes up time and space, has discernible external boundaries, and yet endows the player with a consciousness of timelessness, with an experience outside the everyday lifeworld that partakes of infinity.
>
> (Stewart 1978: 120)

The strategies that artists employ can be seen as a play with space and time and, whether they are engaged in speeding it up or generating an excess of movement, their raps draw attention to both temporality and spatiality. The exaggerated arm gestures of the dancers above, along with the MC's use of the rhythm of his lyrics to draw attention to the temporality of language and the thematisation of time, highlight the metacommunicative aspect of rapping. Stewart argues:

> Like any form of ostensive metacommunication, play implicates itself—is caught up in a reflexive and infinite gesture. Its every utterance

undercuts itself and gives us movement without direction, temporality without order.

(Stewart 1978: 119)

Through their privileged position in the dance space, MCs work to change the parameters of the context, making the abstract tangible and producing an experience that moves beyond the temporal order of everyday life.

PRODUCING FUNKY FEMININITIES

The Sidewinder event in Bristol's O2 Academy, in February 2009, provides a useful example with which to discuss the relation between rap and the body. Although the event was not held in London, the artists involved were based in the capital. The Bristol event is useful within the scope of the study of London-based rap because the Sidewinder brand was recognisable within London's grime scene, and a number of prominent artists within the scene performed. These included Scratchy, of Roll Deep, and the so-called God-father of Grime, Wiley. While each club night is unique, in that the place, time, audience, performers, and the selection of music are never the same, this event also possessed a number of similarities to the majority of large events that I attended during the period of nightclub-based ethnography in London.

Prior to dealing with common practices that were also observed in other venues, I want to analyse how femininity was materialised in this particular event through a grotesque aesthetic. During the early stages of this night the DJ played Sticky's 'Booo!' featuring Miss Dynamite's vocals. As this garage tune played and Dynamite was heard repeating the phrase 'hitemwit-dadrum,' the MC on the stage called to the audience: 'Ladies, I wanna see your bums touch the floor.' The topographical inversion involved interpel-lating the young women on the dance floor as 'ladies,' with the cultural and class connotations that the word carries. This was followed by travestying the concept through referring to their bums. The shift from high to low was then reinforced by asking them to touch the floor. This vulgar linguistic play was followed later that night with the more complex and ambivalent perfor-mance of a young white woman dancing vigorously. She repeatedly adjusted her clothing, but never slowed the pace of her movement. Her energetic performance and somewhat revealing attire articulated an ambivalence of sexual and physical freedom with complicity in the sexualisation of females within the dominant culture and the demands of the male gaze. In order to engage with the complexity of this performance I want to draw upon Caro-lyn Cooper's defence of 'slackness' against Gilroy's charge of its political conservatism. In *There Ain't No Black in the Union Jack* Gilroy describes slackness as 'crude and often insulting wordplay pronouncing on sexuality and sexual antagonism' (2002: 252) that developed in Jamaican dance hall culture in the 1980s. In response to this assessment, Cooper argues:

> [Slackness] can be seen to represent part of a radical, underground confrontation with the patriarchal gender ideology and pious morality of fundamentalist Jamaican society. In its invariant coupling with Culture, Slackness is potentially a politics of subversion. For slackness is not mere sexual looseness—though it certainly is that. Slackness is a metaphorical revolt against law and order; an undermining of consensual standards of decency. It is the antithesis of culture.
>
> (Cooper 1993: 141)

Sociological conceptions of culture simply as what people do, without regards to the notion of the 'best,' can slip into ignorance of the processes of cultural development. Without accepting Cooper's opposition of slackness to culture entirely, I suggest that slackness may be thought of as an overturning of, or withdrawing from, particular ideals within a culture. The slackening of constraints directed to particular forms of propriety may potentially allow previously impossible forms of engagement, or the reemergence of repressed relations. I want to highlight the continuing importance of effort in relation to notions of 'sweetness and light' (Arnold 2006) and, consequently, how slackness may be understood as a revolt against dominant social and cultural values.

Within this analytic frame, the young woman's performance may be seen as both complicit within and in revolt against the dominant culture. Through Bourdieu's (1984: 179) analysis of the body as the materialisation of class taste, the energetically mobile body of this young woman may be considered alongside the MC's topographical inversion, as opposed to dominant norms. In her movements and physical form she conducts herself as a bon vivant, 'someone capable of entering into the generous and familiar—that is, both simple and free—relationship that is encouraged and symbolized by eating and drinking together, in a conviviality which sweeps away restraints and reticence.' The conviviality, of which her dancing body is a material manifestation, is not in this case produced through her eating habits. Her disposition is manifested through her body's movements in response to the soundscape.

In his study of wining in Trinidad, Daniel Miller reports that his female informants state that 'the dance uses the idiom of sexuality rather than being "about" sexuality, in that they describe their experience of the music and dance in terms of a more general feeling of a release from pressure' (1991: 335). I want to draw a connection between the vigorous movements of the young woman as she danced separately to, but near, her black female friend and Miller's argument that low-income 'Bacchanal' women objectify 'Absolute Freedom' through the embodied action of wining and the idiom of autosexuality. The rhythm of the music that she danced to and the MCing that urged her on enabled her body, with others, to revolt against 'law and order' at a material and symbolic level. She developed and reproduced a disposition that preserves elements of freedom that can also be seen within particular forms of rapping. This aesthetic work was achieved through efforts directed away from refinement towards perfection, and through vigorous gestures unconcerned with the cultivation of the dominant forms of individualist femininity.

Judith Butler's critique of Bourdieu is valuable here. She argues that his emphasis on the authority of the authorised speaker in the efficacy of speech acts overlooks how the expropriability of dominant discourse 'constitutes one potential site of its subversive resignification' (Butler 1999: 123). Her example that being 'called a "girl" from the inception of existence is a way in which the girl becomes transitively "girled" over time' (Butler: 120) draws attention to the force of nonofficial, everyday illocutionary acts. MCs' calls and the linguistic and bodily responses of their audiences produce an antiphonic structure. With this antiphony in mind, Austin's contention that the 'performance of an illocutionary act involves the securing of *uptake*' (Austin: 117, emphasis in text) may be considered alongside Butler's argument that the 'body does not merely act in accordance with certain regularized or ritualized practices, but it *is* this sedimented ritual activity; its action, in this sense, is a kind of incorporated memory' (Butler: 115, emphasis in text). The uptake that we are concerned with in relation to this MC's speech is one that is registered in the young woman's body.

It is necessary to consider how Miss Dynamite's repeated reference to the materiality of music—'hitemwitdadrum'—and the live MC's references to the body may have a social force which summons a particular form of identification from this young woman. The DJ's demand was not responded to literally: she did not place her bottom on the dance floor. However, I argue that through her movements in that social space, the dispositions of a funky femininity were materialised in response to the MC's summons. In Miller's analysis of wining in the Trinidadian Carnival, he states that 'for a minority it represents a crystallization rather than an inversion of values. In this case what is enacted is essentially a sexuality which does not require men; it is not lesbianism but auto-sexuality' (1991: 333). I suggest that, as a consequence of the social force of the MC's perlocutionary act, the young woman engaged in a bodily exploration of freedom through the idiom of sexuality. The MC's raps solicit identification from the audience, and her performance was expressive of the production of a feminine identity in response to that call. Together, MCs, DJs, and dancers conjure cultural relations and identities in a ritualised exploration of the freedom that this space offers. In the context with which Miller was concerned, the oppressive sexual relations that he observed justified his 'invocation of the notion of "Absolute Freedom"' in order to identify the negation of everything that binds the individual to the social world. I suggest that this young woman's dancing body and the vulgar raps were involved in a serious play that produces alternatives to the existing, militarised social order.

'DIGITAL KINESIS'

The work of MCs, whether in cyphers or on stage, is valued not so much for its semantic content as for its social function. As I have shown above, performative speech acts and bodily movements solicit and enact identification. Through this antiphonic structure, identities are produced and explored in the black public sphere. These strategies may be mobilised in the subversion of the processes through which dominant social groups represent, criminalise, marginalise, and commodify black culture. Forces operating outside of the space of the dance may be resignified through linguistic and bodily practices. A processual understanding of the aura radically changes how we understand the rap 'text.' I provide a close reading of Dizzee Rascal's 'Sirens' in the following chapter, but want to *détourné* that reading here by drawing attention to how that 'text' may be transformed in the dance space. In this way I want to show how the use of rap embodies a principle that the 'artwork's integrity as object should never outweigh the possibilities for continuing creation through use of that object' (Shusterman 1991: 618). The rap song becomes productive, rather than a product.

At a 'Milkshake' event in the Ministry of Sound on December 16, 2008, Zane Lowe appeared as a guest DJ. During the high point of his set the DJ played 'Sirens,' but radically 'cut and mixed' it. Dizzee's vocals were played over a guitar-based rock track, defamiliarising them from their context within the music video or with the instrumentals on the album recording. After the first verse, Lowe repeatedly played Dizzee's warning—'I can hear the siren's coming'—while mixing it with KRS-One's 'woop, woop' from the chorus of 'Sound of da Police.' The effect was to heighten the audience's response to the soundscape that Lowe produced, by overlaying these artists upon one another and the instrumental backing. The audience cheered, danced in their groups, and thrust their hands in the air as they worked through the sonic shifts and danced to the heavy bass that replaced the guitar instrumental during a segment in which the two MCs' vocals were cut to, back and forth. This soundscape produced a field that inclined dancers' bodies towards particular forms of identification.

At that event, as well as a number of others, I observed groups of dancers forming circles. The members of these groups participated with one another in the production of the aura by working upon the cultural resources brought to bear upon the dance space by DJs, MCs, and other dancers. In relation to this, Peter contrasts the way that he shouts 'in people's faces,' when on his own, with dancing in a group, noting that 'there's some tunes where people get in a circle' in which participants 'spit the lyrics at the same time.' For him these circles produce 'not friendship, but it shows that, yeah, we're in the same group or category and that we all do the same thing.' This emphasis of shared feelings within the circle can be related to Sterling Stuckey's discussion of the ring shout, in which African cosmology was combined with Christian elements in ritual dancing within a circle:

> The intensely religious atmosphere was encouraged by the 'plantation leader,' a figure whose precise religious role was not defined, but who called slaves to praise meetings three evenings a week and 'thrice again on Sundays.' Those among them who moved furthest into Christianity—or led whites to think they had—the ones who seemed to 'distrust the institution [of the ring shout] a little,' found license for it in the Bible, 'which records, they say, that "the angels *shout* in heaven."'
>
> (Stuckey 1987: 86, emphasis and parenthesis in text)

Stuckey's discussion of the circle's role in ancestor worship and spirit possession may be used to understand how religious practices associated with the summoning of spirits have been adapted to the conjuring of identity in the contemporary black public sphere. Peter continues, '. . . because we're in the circle we'd all be, like, shouting *within* the circle. So its kind of like to everyone. Everyone shouts to everyone within the circle' (Peter's emphasis). While the circle's formal similarity to religious ritual may be seen through rap's historical relation to slave culture, its profaned form in the commercial context of the nightclub reveals how the appropriation of this cultural practice is reorganised in its contemporary urban context. A coarse materiality can be observed in the repetition of noises. The emphasis on tone over semantic meaning, as well as rap music's vulgar lyrical content, also suggest a link with the festivity of the Bakhtinian banquet. This quality can also be noted in the bodily practices exercised on the dance floor: 'Freedom and equality are expressed in familiar blows, a coarse bodily contact. Beatings are . . . a tangible equivalent of improper speech' (Bakhtin 1984: 246). Whether they are concerned with the construction of funky femininities or the exploration of a temporality 'deep down inside the bush,' the bodily responses to MCs' lyrics form part of a social continuum. The continued use of this practice suggests the enduring value of this cultural form in its role in producing collective identification and providing resources of hope in postcolonial London.

The coarse materiality of Bakhtinian festivity was visible during my observation at the Academy in Bristol and an event at Matter on July 31, 2009. At that event a group of young men pushed and shoved one another as they danced together. Importantly, their actions did not result in fighting. The familiar bodily contact was sustained for a substantial amount of time (almost the entire duration of Boy Better Know's performance). Rather than describing this as 'violence,' it is more appropriate to relate the shifts between their pushing and shoving, their jumping together with arms around one another's shoulders, and their turning towards each other in a circle to perform gestures that punctuate the rhythms of the rap lyrics to the embodied identification with the MCs' work.

The Bristol Academy and Matter events were structured as live PAs around MCs performing on the stage. Rappers faced the audience, who stood in front of and below them, while DJs were positioned behind the MC. At Matter and a BiggaFish promotion at the London Astoria, the organisation of the MCs seemed to promote a coarse, bodily excitement within the audience. The crews, in particular Boy Better Know at Matter and Nu Brand Flexx at the Astoria, moved around the stage rapidly, interacting with other performers and urging the crowd to move through their gestures. Although they were separated and elevated from the audience by the stage, the combined activities of the audience and MCs produced affective identifications. At Matter and the Bristol Academy, I observed members of the audience turning from the stage in order to interact with other members of the audience or to dance alone amongst the crowd. This behaviour occurred mainly amongst those who were involved in the coarse, bodily contact discussed above. The turning away from the staged performance is a material recognition of the self as part of a larger performance. Consequently, the acts of everyone shouting to and being in physical contact with everyone may be considered material and linguistic manifestations of the primary purpose of these events, rather than as secondary to the rap performance on stage. Without doubt, by turning away from the stage, dancers severed the oracular link between themselves and the artists performing. In this movement, material-linguistic identification is privileged over the visual or spectacular.

In contrast to the actions of the audience at the PA events, in every club night I attended in which rap music was played, groups within the audience would dance in circles. During the nightclub ethnography I spent some time focussing on one particular club, the Ministry of Sound. In successive events I observed young men and women dancing in circles, or in pairs, often rapping the lyrics of the songs they danced to. In some circles the dance incorporated the gestures observed in music videos; in others dancers stooped low, gesturing forwards with their hands. In one particular event, on August 26, 2008, I observed a circle of boys and girls dancing to Donaeo's 'Afrikan Warrior.' The members danced vigorously, dipping low and gesturing with their hands. However, I was surprised to observe that after the song came to an end the group broke up, walking away from one another, and that the individual members seemed not to have previously known the others in the circle. Peter recalls that 'in some cases, in fact in most cases the circle will form because someone might know a few people who are around as well. And then I think that acts as a catalyst and attracts other people, people who were feeling the same thing, to form the circle.' He highlights the common occurrence of circles being formed amongst people who are unfamiliar with one another, stating that he does it 'all the time.' Peter also suggested that participating in these cultural forms produces a feeling of commonality and sameness: 'We still wouldn't know each other but we know that we have something in common. So you know, if I was to pass by someone who I was in the circle with earlier I'd be like "oh, cool." You know, just be safe.' The circle enables the collective affirmation of a class disposition, sharing feelings of sameness and reproducing a familiarity essential to the continuation of London's black culture. These affirmations of a convivial culture are produced both linguistically and through physical gesture. Sarah Thornton argues that black-British music cultures 'often emphasize the strength of communities outside the dance club setting, seeing the "vibe" as an affirmation of a politicized black identity' (1995: 30). In slackening the constraints of urban dwelling, the vulgarity of these temporary autonomous zones enables the exploration of ways to be together that the formality of the dominant cultural mode does not permit.

'WHAT DO YOU KNOW ABOUT VIOLENCE?'

This study was conducted during a period of widespread media speculation about 'gang violence' and 'knife crime' in London. As some of this news coverage attempted to link grime to that violence,[3] I want to deal with grime and its political, economic, and social contexts more fully than I am able within the present discussion of the aura. I will therefore leave that broader discussion to chapter five, where I can relate the issue of violence to the economic and political concerns of artists and their publics. However, I will use this space to consider some aspects of what may be perceived as violence and its relation to the social process of rapping. Before doing so it is necessary to state that the print, radio, and television media's association of grime with 'violence' and knife crime limits the ways in which we see the black body and black culture more broadly. Bourdieu highlights the 'specifically political effects of moralization' through what he terms 'the new therapeutic morality.' He argues:

> The most fundamental principles of class identity and unity, those which lie in the unconscious, would be affected if, on the decisive point of relation to the body, the dominated class came to see itself only through the eyes of the dominant class, that is, in terms of the dominant definition of the body and its uses.
>
> (Bourdieu 1984: 384)

Whereas Bourdieu was concerned with the effect of 'challenges to working-class identification with virility' on the French peasantry's diminished ability to define 'the principles of its own identity,' I am concerned with the challenges to urban, working-class identities, especially those of young men and women. Within the context of the militarisation of everyday life, racially discriminatory policing practices, and the association of rap music with antisocial behaviour, violence, and criminality in the mainstream media, it is important to open up the ways in which we understand how the body, gesture, and unconscious urges are explored through their relation to this music. Through such a strategy it may be possible to identify how MCs and DJs organise a collective resistance to the stigmatisation of the working class and enable their audiences to construct oppositional identities.

It is clear from Peter's statements that he experiences through some grime music a form of catharsis. In the ritualistic rapping and dancing to 'Pow!,' repressed feelings may be brought to the surface and dissipated. However, it is also apparent from his statements that these powerfully felt urges may not always be contained within the cultural forms that have been developed to express them. DJs stated that their usual method of dealing with the possibility of violent conflict is to follow a track such as Lethal B's 'Pow!' with either a different genre or a grime track that would not heighten the physical response further. The DJs employ their 'aesthetic agency' (Witkin and De Nora 1997: 5) and organise these events in a manner that aims to contain the possibility of violent, physical conflict by allowing the audience to release its energy in a controlled manner. Johnson's discussion of Jamaican music's cathartic qualities is relevant to these confrontations:

> The dances which complement the popular music . . . are at once erotic and sensual, violent, aggressive and cathartic. . . . But it so happens that, at times, the catharsis does not come through dance, for the violence that the music carries is turned inwards and personalized, so that for no apparent reason, the dance halls and yards often explode into fratricidal violence and general pandemonium. Whenever two rival sound systems meet, violence often erupts between the rival supporters, so the dj is often both the musical pace setter and the musical peace keeper. He tells the dancers, 'those who deal in violence shall go down in silence.'
>
> (Johnson 1976: 400)

The sensual qualities of the music combine with the role of dance in facilitating the expression of subjective experience and a collective release of suppressed emotions, which may potentially precipitate physical violence. This highlights the efficacy of the MCs and DJs' performances in soliciting identification and their production of collective 'emotional states' (De Nora 1999). However, it also requires them to carefully orchestrate the audience's response. That orchestration may operate through the selection of songs that will not further heighten aroused passions or, in the strategy that Johnson identifies in Jamaican popular music culture, the MC's direct appeal to the audience: 'The dub-lyricist who has developed the dj talk into a form of music-poetry, tells his listeners that they are invited to a musical happening, but he warns them, "when you come/I don't want you to bring your skeng/I want you to leave your skeng at home." '[4] There is a self-regulation at work in rap music scenes that is directed towards avoiding violence, while not avoiding the problematic of dealing with 'violent' urges.

Before continuing this discussion of the control exercised in London's contemporary rap culture, it is worth pausing to consider Richard Wright's discussion of culture and identity in the 'literature of the American Negro.' Wright outlines his use of two concepts that he opposes to one another: 'Entity, men integrated with their culture; and identity, men who are at odds with their culture, striving for personal identification' (2008: 738). In his analysis of black American writing he contrasts Phyllis Wheatley (who he saw as integrated with her culture) with poets, such as George Horton, whose work conveys 'a sense of distance between him and the land in which he lives' (Wright 2008: 742). Wright's discussion is relevant to London's grime scene because of his attentiveness to the changing social conditions in which black cultural expression was produced. He describes the intent of the Dozens as jeering 'at life; they leer at what is decent, holy, just, wise, straight, right, and uplifting' and states that this profane form sums up 'the mood of despairing rebellion' (2008: 755). I will consider some Dozens lyrics in detail in the following chapter. However, I want to draw attention to this cultural form here because of the role of such profane lyrics in generating the 'hype' of the circles that MCs and DJs refer to and the potential for 'violence' to be expressed. The Dozens manifests the pressures faced by young blacks in the capital and dramatises the confrontation with such social forces.

In H. 'Rap' Brown's discussion of the mother and sister rhyming that occurs in the Dozens, he describes social and economic conditions in which 'you'd be walking down the street one night and some white dude in a car would pull up next to you and say, "hey, boy, you got a sister?"' (Brown 1993: 356). The mother-rhyming of the Dozens that he participated in was related to the pimping and prostitution that was prevalent in American ghettos. Following Brown's description of the Dozens as 'a mean game because what you try to do is totally destroy somebody with words' (1993: 354), I argue that this is part of a process through which young people learn to bear the pressures to which they are subject. In the context of Brown's mother-rhyming, cultural practices developed in Africa were adapted to a situation in which the incest taboo was travestied by the wider society. To castigate the practice of mother-rhyming by black men without considering the social context in which that practice takes place is not simply irresponsible. Such an approach reinforces the unjust relations that lead to these ritualised releases of pressure. This black cultural practice dramatises the social pressures faced by this subordinated group and offers the opportunity to construct an identity capable of dealing with those forces.

It is important to bear this role in mind when considering how this cultural form is adapted and used in postcolonial London's grime scene. JJ and Peter both discussed incidents of unjust treatment by the police. Whereas JJ described being stopped without just cause by the police on several occasions,

Peter described an incident in which he witnessed two police officers observing his friend at a train station as that friend saw his girlfriend off. Once she boarded the train and departed the police officers approached the young man. They then conducted a search of Peter's friend, which involved the humiliation of having him remove his upper garments and expose his body in public. Seeker's work with children and young adults led him to become concerned about the use of 'stop and search' powers by the police:

> If you're pulled over on a high street it can be one of the most embarrassing things, especially when you haven't done anything. You know, if you can clearly see that the police are taking advantage then you're not gonna be very pleased. . . . You're first instinct is to think 'I haven't done anything, I'm going about my business and this person has stopped me. Why? Because they can.' So what happens is a power trip can kick in on the police side and then also on the young people's side a need to lash out, which can result in an innocent young person getting arrested for no reason.

Themes of brutality in rap music are employed in a process through which young people learn to deal with the forces that structure everyday life in the city. This often takes the form of resisting jeers at themselves and acquiring the ability to return 'as good as they got.' Dancers also use the sensual qualities of the music to allow repressed urges to resurface and dissipate.

Johnson's discussion of the cathartic quality of Jamaican popular music refers to Frantz Fanon's analysis of colonised cultures: 'The occupier, in fact, likened these scathing denunciations, outpourings of misery, and heated words to an act of catharsis. Encouraging these acts would, in a certain way, avoid dramatisation and clear the atmosphere' (Fanon 2004: 173). The experiences of unjust policing should draw our attention to the *colonial* character of life in postcolonial London. Neither 'violent' lyrics nor 'violent' behaviour within London's youth cultures will substantially change until the lived experience of young people changes. By collectively exploring their experiences through song and dance urban youths already deal with much of the pressure that could potentially result in outbursts of physical violence. The acts of catharsis have an important role in accommodating young, working-class men and women to their position in the wider social whole.

Peter's reference to 'pretend' confrontations within the dance space highlights the social function of rap in staging scenes in which emotions are dealt with in a productive manner. Such performances enact the primal scene Fanon describes, in which the black man seeks recognition of his humanity (Fanon 2007: 191–197). 'If there's no fights then, its just gestures really . . . pretend fighting, no, no—pretend—if you can imagine someone coming up to you and saying "oh what? What? You got a problem?" In your face kind of thing. But it's not actually meant, its just during, its just during the actual song.' The avoidance of violence by Peter and the vast majority of young adults in grime events suggests that music, rapping, and dance are generally sufficient to contain the 'violent' urges of those who need to express them: 'Because of the vibe that the tune gives out, it makes everyone feel like they've got power, and so they like to let it out. But because everyone knows that its just the tune, no-one really gets—well some people do get mad, I don't know why they do get mad, but usually people know that its just a joke.' Peter's experience of grime music as aiding the dissipation rather than the precipitation of 'violence' suggests rap music has a significant role in socialising subjective experience and organising the audience's consciousness. It is important to bear in mind that 'violence' is only one of the issues that rap is employed to deal with in contemporary London. Among those other issues, it also confronts racist oppression, as well as the production of subaltern black identities. The means through which MCs and DJs organise the collective consciousness of their audiences and the manner in which members of the audience work through their subjective feelings highlight how rap provides an important entry point into underlying socioeconomic and political issues.

JJ's discussion of the difference between the 'Shoreditchy crowd,' which frequently attends grime events, and those that would have attended his youth centre is relevant to this issue, and what he describes as incidences of 'madness' in clubs:

> I think them Shoreditchy people are a lot more free—than the people that come from my youth centre would have been. . . . In the sense that they all bubble, if someone looks at them they won't hype like. Dunno, you stare at a man too much in the youth centre back in the day it would have been a lot for you in the youth centre, innit.

In one of the events in which he observed the two crowds mix, as happened 'from time to time' in the grime scene, he recalled: 'It was alright. But you know what it was, you saw how timid the Shoreditchy crowd was around them kind of people. That's the only thing I would definitely say. They weren't as relaxed as they normally was. They weren't as loud as they normally was.' Significantly JJ insisted that the 'youth centre' crowd do not cause 'madness' and are not to blame for it, but 'they can relate to it a lot better—'cause I would say they are around it a lot more than them Shoreditchy crowd people are.' He continues: 'They can relate to it on a level where they see it a lot more and its not gonna faze them as much. But in a sense of—boy how they deal with it, they deal with it extremely different to how the Shoreditchy crowd would deal with it.' Johnson's discussion of the naming of Jamaican popular music may be useful in the consideration of JJ's use of the terms—free, timid, relaxed, madness, and being fazed: 'The youth sufferers who live in the ghettoes and shanty towns of Jamaica describe the music in terms of their own existence: they call the music *rebel music* . . . and this is so precisely because the music is expressive of how they "feel"' (Johnson 1976: 399). The rebel music is expressive of forces that produce subjectivities such as 'I Roy's "screw-face man" . . . the man who has completely internalized the historical experience of violence and the violence of his existence, and acts this out through an existence of violence' (1976: 401).

The term grime conveys a sense of ingrained dirt, or of being blackened through repeated contact with dirt. It is significant that this term was used as an aesthetic quality and later taken up to identify the music that was produced by the 'youth centre' crowd that JJ described. The term is expressive of the process of racialisation or the acquisition of a *habitus* through experiences of unfreedom in London and having to face up to these. JJ's contrast between these two groups highlights the exploration of freedom through grime and the subjectivities formed though familiarity with experiences of particular kinds of tension, of which the music is expressive.

Concluding this discussion of rap's role in the socialisation of 'violent' urges, I want to consider the formal mechanisms through which this occurs. When discussing their interest in grime with a group of A-Level students, one directed me to a YouTube clip. The video, *Dizzee Rascal vs Crazy Titch*, was used by him as an example of the grime scene's violence. In the video, it was possible to see a breakdown in the order of the staged encounter, or 'battle,' between these artists. However, rather than showing any actual physical violence, what I observed in this scene was the exercise of self-restraint following this breakdown. I later discussed the video with the student after watching it. My examination of its content proceeded through conversations with other members of the grime scene. During this process I noticed an overemphasis on violence as a constituent feature of the scene amongst listeners and a sensitivity amongst artists to the scene being represented as violent.

A principle of order governing the structure of the 'battle' can be identified in this video. The exercise of masculine self-restraint by the participants following the breakdown of that order was a significant sociocultural performance in this event. The video shows physical contact and verbal confrontation between the two antagonists. Importantly, this assertion of their masculinity does not develop into physical violence. During the prolonged face off between the artists there is a substantial amount of physical contact amongst the onlookers and between onlookers and the two artists. That material reassurance of belonging was accompanied with calls for the artists to 'allow that' and disregard the breach of order. The reassuring physical contact between the participants in this scene should not be overlooked in the consideration of how young, black men deal with the social forces that act upon them.

The breach was caused by Titch turning towards Dizzee as if to pass him the microphone, then turning away from him and continuing to rap his lyrics while retaining possession of the mic. Dizzee responds to this by pushing him and, in the subsequent stand off, repeatedly asserting, 'I'm not a mook.' That the offence was caused by this foregrounds the principle of reciprocal recognition that constitutes the underlying order of this collective performance.

In contrast to the cypher, in which a rapper is likely to have to deal with the vexation of being cut off by another at any moment, this confrontation results from the reciprocal structure of the encounter being disrupted. In opposition to JJ's claim that anyone could be involved in the 'madness' that might occur through rap music, I suggest that the music is expressive of the social pressures and subjective feelings of a particular marginalised group. Consequently, members of that social group are more likely to be involved in the manifestation of 'violence.' What I want to emphasise here is not whether or not violence is present in particular rap scenes, but that the social relations that are produced through rapping are directed towards reciprocity and collaboration. Furthermore, I argue in opposition to H. 'Rap' Brown, who remains in the position of one of the players in his description of the Dozens, that 'violence' is produced in the breach of these relations and not as their aim, which is to develop linguistic and bodily control and to produce social identity. Clearly, the assertiveness that is expressed in Dizzee and Titch's performances of masculinity has the potential to shift towards actual, physical violence. Just as importantly, this possibility is also contained by and dissipated through the physical contact amongst members of the assembled group.

When considering this potential for violence, it is necessary to bear in mind the character of London's postcoloniality, as well as how cultural resources are employed to deal with the conditions of urban dwelling that give rise to such urges. In light of the overemphasis on and sensitivity to 'violence' amongst those in the grime scene, it may be possible to discern the expression of social being through the idiom of violence in the way that the video is used, if not in the event recorded by the video itself. Even if what the video shows is a principle of reciprocity (which, when breached, gives way to masculine self-assertion, self-restraint, physical reassurance, and collective being), the idiom of violence has considerable interpretative power in this scene. It is necessary to emphasise the importance of this problematic, as the video's 'violence' perhaps also holds the potential of developing nonviolent and affirmative social relations.

THE ORGANISATION OF THE COLLECTIVE BODY

In nightclubs across the capital dancers may perform gestures that mimetically identify with those recorded by artists in music videos. This occurred significantly less than the formation of circles in the events that I attended. However, the practice highlights a cultural context that goes beyond the walls of the nightclub. In addition to the 'Rolex Sweep,' the 'Migraine

Skank' became a recognisable feature of London's nightclub scene during the course of this study. The dance was popularised by Gracious K (a member of Red Hot) through an instructional video circulated via YouTube. The video combines oral directions with visual demonstration, which supplements the instructional content of the lyrics: 'First step is take your right hand, next step is take your left hand, and then put both hands on the head, and then show me the migraine skank.' The video assists the introduction of a novel pattern of movements into contemporary black popular culture. It also contains recognition of a common fund of embodied knowledge within the dance culture: 'Anyone here who goes to a rave knows about going down low.' Gracious K's skank incorporates elements of the preexisting cultural tradition and contributes to that culture. Following the dance's popularisation in nightclubs across the capital, Afrikan Boy performed a gesture recognisable as part of the migraine skank (moving the palm of the hand around the head) during the freestyle section of 'Kunta Kinte.' At this stage in its 'life cycle' the skank had become detached from the 'text' of the video and used as material for the continuation and revitalisation of the culture from which it emerged. The process of production, internalisation, and adaptation of cultural signs may be seen as a common feature of rap scenes. In this process the changing practices through which appropriation takes place is of paramount importance, as opposed to the integrity of the 'text.' Afrikan Boy's incorporation of a particular gesture from the skank into his own freestyle dancing may be considered alongside the performance of slackness as part of the exploration of black human possibilities in these spaces. His performance helps to engage with the dynamic interplay between sound, text, and body in the production of identity and identification in the black public sphere.

Through Afrikan Boy's comments on the power of music and poetry it is possible to draw out a connection between his creative practice and the process of soliciting identification from the audience:

> When you listen to like a slow jam, while you just feel heart broken. Like there's certain tracks that you feel they've witnessed everything that's happened to you and they're just singing it. But obviously they haven't, you know. And its just like that's the power that music or poetry or sort of anything like has, even adverts. You know there's some people that watch adverts and think 'aah they're talking to me' and then go out and do whatever the advert says.

His association of advertising, music, and poetry with the idea of 'witnessing' one's feelings, experiences, or subjectivity draws attention to the grounded aesthetics of his own creative work. In contrast to the apparently simplified example of 'some people's' relation to adverts that Afrikan Boy presents, Paul Willis highlights how advertisements may be considered by their audiences to be 'expressive forms capable of giving symbolic pleasure, whose ability to produce pleasure can be evaluated' (1990: 50). Afrikan Boy's alternation between what 'you feel' and the 'obviousness' of artifice is suggestive of the complex relationships that are constituted between audiences and particular cultural forms, such as music, poetry, and television adverts. The ironic relation to these forms that he constructs through the figure of 'some people' foregrounds the interplay between identification with lyrics and the performance of identities constructed through black cultural representations. His comments are suggestive of his approach to the organisation of the collective consciousness of his audience. The use of the term 'witness' suggests a relation between him and the audience through which he summons identification in order that they attest to a truth. This may be considered as the audience's ability to take up his solicitation and produce identities that correspond to his performance.

After accepting a beat offered to him by a producer, Afrikan Boy 'attacked it in many different ways' before the name Kunta Kinte came to mind.[5] After using YouTube to find clips from the TV series, he experimented with working his lyrics, the sampled clip, and the beat together. There is clearly much work done and intentionality exercised by Afrikan Boy. However, the creative process also had an aspect that appeared to come from outside of that intention: 'I decided . . . let me see what happens when I carry on playing the Kunta Kinte clip until my . . . verse starts. And what's so weird is when . . . you carry on playing the clip. . . . And the minute he says "it's Toby" that's when my verse starts and I was like "wow, this track is just meant to be."' The creative development of this track also took place through performance, initially in private—'I like writing my lyrics standing up, so I always try to perform my lyrics whilst I'm creating them'—and then in public:

> When I go on stage the performance influences . . . Fairfield Halls was the first time I performed it, everyone loved it. . . . Everyone loves that track. I've done it in two clubs . . . I think what grabs people is the way I say the lyrics but more so the performance . . . I like that track, I'm gonna record it next week. It's not even recorded yet, that's how fresh it is.

The honing of the rap through a combination of private and public performance before recording it is an important aspect of the social creativity of London's rap scenes. It is possible to see, in Afrikan Boy's experimentation with video and encounters with his audiences, the refinement of the process of soliciting identification. Afrikan Boy's experimentation with video on his computer and offering of his reinterpretation of that clip to his audience highlights the role of rap in an ongoing social process of experimentation, appropriation, and affirmation.

The social creation of 'Kunta Kinte' is linked to the collective purpose for which Afrikan Boy wrote his lyrics. He adopts the persona of the fictional, enslaved African in his performance: 'I'm gonna make a track and I'm gonna do it like I am Kunta Kinte.' The Kunta Kinte persona was adapted to a contemporary setting, combining the background of the film's Kunta with Afrikan Boy's contemporary cultural references:

That's where the 'praise be to Allah' comes in, cause obviously where Kunta Kinte's from in the film its like 99% Muslim. . . . So then I wrote the track like I'm Kunta Kinte but I done it in a weird way like I'm sort of like a modern day Kunta Kinte, but I sort of like flip back to all them back references, like: 'My name is Kunta Kinte, I don't drive a hummer but I get many whips from my old slave masters/ Praise be to Allah, thank Jesus for Obama.'

By sampling the scene of Kunta Kinte being broken, and then drawing out the theme of 'being yourself,' Afrikan Boy develops a complex historicism that combines digital technology, a nonlinear temporality, and references to African, black-American, and European culture. The mixed 'race,' but predominantly white, audience at his performance in the Notting Hill Arts Centre responded by chanting back the lyrics and dancing. This active reception is part of the process of organising a collective consciousness that is aware of the history of racial terror, but focussed on the production of affirmative ways of living together today. The playing of Bob Marley's 'Redemption Song' immediately after 'Kunta Kinte' at this performance is one way in which the rapper offers the audience a means of dealing with the issues raised in his lyrics. The heavy beat and the low light, in which he performs his rap and the dancers move, was followed by a stillness as Marley's guitar gently plays.

CONCLUSION

As I draw to a conclusion, I want to consider a group of young women at the Sidewinder event. Dancing in a circle, the three white women, with one young man, gestured to Donaeo's 'African Warrior' in a similar manner to the group described above, with the exception that they did not dip down as that group had. Although the young man appeared distracted, the women's movements and gestures were visibly more engaged with the music. Just as white and Asian MCs participate in London's rap scenes, it is important to consider how white and Asian dancers participate in the reproduction of the conviviality of this culture. In their embodied identification with 'African Warrior,' these young women engaged in a process of cultural interpretation and identity construction that produces a larger, sensual collectivity and a convivial culture that prioritises reciprocal recognition.

The movement of dancing bodies in response to the MC and DJ's performances in a collective appropriation of this black cultural tradition activates the aura in this fading public sphere. I prefer the term 'Master of Ceremonies' to characterise the role that rappers occupy in this sphere. But the appellation of 'Mic Controller,' used by grime MCs, has the merit of identifying the impact of technology on social relations in this scene. The use of recordings and amplified sound transports the MC's voice to clubs throughout the city and beyond. Nevertheless, in the profaned sphere of the rave, the audience's symbolic actions are not mechanically controlled by MCs or DJs. The assembled gathering affirms, rejects, and reinterprets the work offered by figures such as Donaeo, Gracious K, and Afrikan Boy. To be sure, the recording and amplification of these sonic artworks narrows the distance between the MCs and their public. Their audience is able to engage in a tactile appropriation of the rap soundscape through dance and, in their own rapping and chanting, adopt the enunciative position of the MC. MCs and DJs are able to draw upon this technologically mediated relationship to orchestrate the audience's collective exploration of racialised human possibilities.

Through the passions invested in this space, Londoners are empowered to respond to the conditions in which they dwell. These responses include the symbolic overcoming of racist oppression, the exploration of gendered subjectivities, the bodily play on abstract concepts such as time and space, and the production of collective identification. 'Funky femininities' and 'reassuring masculinities' are only two examples of the identities that are produced through the appropriation of cultural resources that are circulated within this public sphere. The performances within the dance space cannot be separated from the social and economic relations within postcolonial London. Through the repetition of noises and lyrics, as well as the movement of their bodies, audiences give expression to their collective feelings and aesthetically explore the freedom granted in this space. The reworking of cultural material in these events also enables the production of substantive identities that may be employed to deal with unjust social relations outside the dance space. The combined efforts of the participants produce a form of communicative action that challenges, subverts, and turns away from the hegemonic representations of the dominant social groups responsible for their stigmatisation and marginalisation. Although MCs and DJs occupy privileged positions within this space, it is through the audiences' relation to their work that the aura is activated in London's black public sphere.

NOTES

1. Peter is not the actual name of the young man interviewed.
2. The MPA's report into the use of the form stated: 'It was concluded that requesting the music style was at best unnecessary and at worst had potential to be perceived as racially discriminatory' and that 'the "make-up of patrons" reference has been removed as it was felt its inclusion could be perceived as potentially racially discriminatory.' http://www.mpa.gov.uk/committees/cep/2009/

091112/09/?qu=Equalities%20Impact%20Assessment%20696&sc=2&ht=1 [Date Accessed 1 April 2010].

3. http://www.thesun.co.uk/sol/homepage/news/2396038/Defoe-brother-dies-after-street-attack.html;
   http://www.thesun.co.uk/sol/homepage/news/2402448/Defoe-brother-suspect-appears-in-court.html;
   http://news.bbc.co.uk/1/hi/uk/6938411.stm [Date Accessed 1 April 2010].

4. '"Skeng" is a Jamaican creolism meaning pistol' (Johnson 1976: 401).

5. Kunta Kinte is a character from the television series *Roots*, first broadcast in 1977, based on Alex Haley's novel *Roots: The Saga of an American Family*. Kunta Kinte is born in Gambia, West Africa, before being captured at the age of 15 by slave traders and transported to America.

4 'That There Kind of Sumthin' Sounds Strange to Me'
Social Representation and the Recorded Soundscape

As I stand in Rhythm Division record shop, in East London's Bow area, JJ recommends J2K's album as a suitable purchase for me on the basis of this artist's lyrical accomplishment. Elaborating upon his statement that J2K is 'one of the best, lyrically,' JJ explains:

> His rhyming patterns, the content of his lyrics. Like what he's actually talking about . . . he doesn't use typical phrases . . . his rhyming pattern's just different, but it stands out a lot, like technically. I can class it lyrically and technically, he's one of the best MCs.

Other criteria that form the grounds of his recommendation of *Wake Up* to me are the 'production' of the tracks and the artist's flow. He states that consideration of the production includes the selection of beats and how the vocals fit into the track. JJ describes flow as a 'beat in a beat' and distinguishes this from lyrical ability and the track's production, in that it concerns 'how you adapt to a beat.' Once considerations of the album's soundtrack are exhausted, he identifies the visual artwork used on its cover as a factor that may influence a purchase. JJ's explanation of the categories that listeners may use draws attention to the modes of perception and appreciation that are acquired through the use of these products in other contexts. Ty states that 'every now and then' people he encounters on the street will 'break down' the lyrics of his songs or talk about his performances. It is clear from both Ty and JJ's comments that formal and thematic analysis is an integral practice in both the grime and UK hip-hop scenes, and a necessary part of the development of particular forms of cultural competence.

The practice of interpreting the thematic and formal qualities of rap songs is also embedded within the songs themselves. Durrty Goodz's 'Switching Songs 2' begins with a quotation of Monstaboy's garage track 'I'm Sorry,' and the MC commences his rapping with the questions 'do you remember them times? Do you remember these days?' The prompt to recollect begins a personal and social history of the grime scene's development, including its emergence from garage. The samples used in the track include references to So Solid Crew's 'Oh No (Sentimental Things),' More Fire Crew's 'Oi,' Dizzee Rascal's 'I Luv U,' and Tinie Tempa's 'Wifey.' The combination of a personal and sociohistorical narrative with this instrumental montage produces a soundscape within which the generation of London's contemporary rap scene is thematised. A further and related theme is the representation of this artist's subjective view of that sociohistorical formation.

The content of rap songs and videos cannot be separated from the social consciousness of those who participate in this city's rap scenes. I want to use this chapter to investigate the relation between rap music products and the interpretative practices of artists and their audiences, by examining the formal and thematic content of these cultural products and performances. The aim of this is not simply to highlight rap's value as an art form (Shusterman 1991: 614), although its literary qualities should certainly be of significance to scholars of contemporary poetry (Bradley 2009: 10–15). Through the development of a critical participant observation I attempt to engage with how the pleasure and popular appeal, which is produced through the combination of the MC's oral poetry and its relation to the music (Bradley: 37–38), are mobilised in the organisation of social being. Although I will focus on the grime scene for the greater part of this discussion, I begin with an examination of the lyrics of a popular track by Roots Manuva. Through a close analysis of these lyrics, which is attentive to their perlocutionary force, I want draw out some of the qualities that anticipate particular responses from his audience. By combining textual analysis with participant observation I aim to probe how lyrics anticipate and produce particular forms of social identification and organisation. Following this, I discuss how certain rhetorical strategies that form a part of the black cultural tradition have been adapted in the production of the grime scene. This leads on to a critical engagement with the representation of racialised and gendered identities in the black public sphere. Finally, I discuss how young, black Londoners' self-representations challenge hegemonic utterances that attempt to stigmatise urban youths and their vernacular culture. Through the analysis of representations of postcolonial London's social and economic order, I attempt to connect MCs' organisation of a social consciousness and the circulation of rap music products to a cultural politics that attempts to overcome the marginalisation of black, urban youth.

TECHNO SHAMANISM

During the course of my research I observed Roots Manuva perform on three occasions. At each event he performed 'Witness (1 Hope),' a track on the *Run Come Save Me* album. His audiences responded by singing the song's lyrics, jumping in unison to the beat, or waving their arms—up and down—to the beat during the chorus. Within this crowd I experience something of a collective pleasure in the bubbling, synthesised beat and the track's driving energy. The popularity of the song facilitates the experience of being part of a moving, collective body, through its performance. 'Witness' begins with a thumping bass line that provides the structure that Roots Manuva's lyrics drive against and that the audience dance (or jump) to. The heavily processed, synthesised effects that accompany the bass line focus the track's energy.

> Taskmaster burst the bionic zit-splitter
> Breakneck speed we drown ten pints of bitter.
> We lean all day and some say that ain't productive
> Could that depend upon the demons that you're stuck with
> Cause right now, I see clearer than most
> I sit here contented with this cheese on toast. I feel the
> Pain of a third world famine. Said way
> We count them blessings and keep jamming. Tis him
> Scumbag, scum of the earth, his worth was nil
> Until he gained the skill of tongues. From fifteen years
> Young straight to my greyback self, I stay
> Top shelf material. Jerk chicken, jerk
> Fish. Breakaway slave, bliss.
> Generate gees and then we stash 'em in the Swiss.
> Fools can't see this, audio pistols. A
> Fistful of hip-hop banzai, progressing in the
> Flesh. Esoteric quotes, most frightening
> Duppy took a hold of my hand while I was writing
> Let go me ting, duppy, let go me hand
> I summon up the power of banana clan!

The first bar of lyrics—'Taskmaster burst the bionic zit splitter'—seems to make no sense whatsoever, but the alliteration works with the bass to produce a pleasing psychosomatic response through the placement of the heavily stressed plosives 'burst' and 'bionic' on the beat. This effect is picked up again at the beginning of the second bar, with 'Breakneck' reaffirming the beat by providing an additional emphasis at the beginning of the new bar, whereas 'bitter' ends the bar by forming a couplet with 'splitter.' The opening of the verse has an energy that drives the audience's response. This is somewhat reduced in the following bars. The third contains an internal rhyme of 'day' with 'say,' and forms a couplet with the fourth through the forced rhyming of 'productive' with 'you're stuck with?' There is a shift in the fifth and sixth lines away from ending the bar with couplets and, although 'most' is rhymed with 'toast,' the next sentence begins within the same bar. This gives 'pain' an additional stress as it is placed at the beginning of the following bar, on the beat. Depending upon how one analyses the lyrics, 'famine' and 'jamming' can be seen as internal rhymes between bars. Alternatively, one could register that, by beginning the following line within the bar of the preceding one, the couplets receive an additional stress by falling on beat, and the space after the beat is taken up by words that do not need an additional emphasis. This allows 'scumbag' to receive an additional stress, which is further emphasised by the repetition of 'scum.'

The repetition of 'jerk' in the references to West Indian cuisine that follow Roots Manuva's assertion that he will stay 'top shelf material' might be associated with the song's concern with the meagre and undervalued. The possible reference to pornography may link bodily responses to such products with the nourishment provided by West Indian food. The theme of poverty and hunger has clearly begun to emerge by this point. The earlier association of 'famine' with 'jamming' suggests music to be a form of sustenance. Later it is represented as a means of economic gain. 'Break away slave bliss' is rhymed with 'Swiss,' and the vernacular reference to banking associates' freedom from dehumanising work with making and saving money. The lines '. . . progressing in the/ Flesh. Esoteric quotes most frightening/ Duppy took a hold of my hand as I was writing' combine the theme of the psychosomatic effects of music with the process of writing. This is formally linked with a concern with spirituality through the couplet 'frightening/writing.' There is a sense, in the performance of these lyrics, that the artist is not entirely in control of the creative process. The experience of surprise at what emerges from this creativity is attached to the word 'Duppy.' The use of the Jamaican word for ghost to refer to the creative process invokes a cultural tradition, and relates it to a struggle with spirit possession. This may in turn be connected to the theme of nourishing food and the references to drug and alcohol use at the beginning of the verse. Rap as part of a cultural tradition, which connects Roots Manuva back to Jamaica, is invoked within the context of a spiritual and bodily struggle within the urban environment, and an engagement with various ways of dealing with that struggle. The song conjures references to drugs (including alcohol), food, rapping, and money-making as means of dealing with life in the city. This theme is returned to in the final verse with the line 'We in collision with the beast/ Lost we religion and we can't get no peace.' There is a suggestion of the tradition's disconnection from the sacred sphere, alongside a celebration of its continuing value in dealing with contemporary urban dwelling.

The chorus allows an increased participation by the audience. After the relative density of language usage towards the end of the first verse and in the later verses, the internal rhyme of 'witness' and 'fitness,' along with the repetition of 'one' in 'One hope, one quest,' allows the pleasure of rhythmic repetition to again become dominant over semantic depth for a few bars. The repetition of the chorus and its privileging of the semiotic contrast with the semantic depth and apparent linearity of the verses. The audience's collective response, moving their bodies and chanting the lyrics in unison, brings about a corporeal solidarity.

A preconscious understanding of the track (including its lyrical and musical aspects) is combined with the presence of the artist, the collective response to his performance, and other environmental factors (such as the dimmed lighting that heightens the audience's nonvisual senses) to produce the truth of 'Witness.' The most significant aspect of this song is the way that its formal qualities anticipate the collective witnessing of the track's unfolding in performance. Each performance is a singular event witnessed by participants in their total communication. In consideration of the role of the audience in the creation of the aura (that I have identified here with the truth of the artwork), it is notable that the majority of Roots Manuva's audiences at the events I have attended are white. The space opened up by this performance explodes essentialised concepts of racial difference. The aura of London's black culture enables an exploration of human sameness through common participation in producing this aura. I argue that Rodney Smith anticipates this audience's response in the composition of his rap music, and that the formal antiphony of 'Witness' is related to the theme of spirit possession and creativity.

Through his performative utterances, Rodney Smith orchestrates the audience's response. His references to food, the body, and spirit, as well as his repeated calls for the audience to 'witness the fitness,' invokes collective identification with the Roots Manuva persona. A collective spirit is summoned, in which the gathering is invited to attest to the MC's fitness. His lyrics urge the audience to attest to a collective truth of their being: whether we hitch hike, or push bike, or travel kind of trash, manifest that with wholesome roots rap. Manifest that, yeah.' Through the use of rhyme and the rhythmic qualities of the lyrics, the rap song works with the beat and other features of the recorded soundscape to elicit a bodily response. The poetic interplay of the lyrics with the heavy beat facilitates the uptake of the song by registering the material qualities of the performance within the body. Smith's sonic organisation of the lyrics in this soundscape highlights the material power of language in this ritual setting. It is through this material dimension that particular forms of identification are solicited by Roots Manuva and produced by the audience. This is then thematically connected to the MC's truthful (re)presentation of the audience's collective experience. Roots Manuva offers this to the audience, providing them with the opportunity to testify to its truth, and through their dancing and chanting the aura is made materially manifest. The track's concern with spirit possession is repeatedly constructed in everyday, material terms. His anticipation and orchestration of the audience's responses may be related to the production of modes of social being in the contemporary urban environment.

SOCIAL REPRESENTATION AND THE GRIME SCENE

Shifting focus from the way that Roots Manuva's song anticipates and is therefore constitutive of the audience's responses, I want to consider two grime 'texts': 'Black Boys' and a clip circulated on YouTube entitled 'Bashy goin at Wiley and Scratchy (live).' They both feature Bashy rapping, and I want to discuss them in connection with the social relations that constitute grime's subaltern public sphere. Although the performance captured in the clip may not have been intended for publication by Bashy, and was recorded prior to the production of 'Black Boys,' I wish to look at the later video first in order to engage with its role in the mainstreaming of black culture. I will then compare it with the position that Bashy takes in the earlier recording.

The 'Black Boys' video, which was also circulated on YouTube, features a sample from the Stairsteps' 'Ooh Child.' Whereas Gilroy (1994: 53) discusses R. Kelly's reference to this song in 'Bump N Grind,' I suggest that the use of this sample here owes more to Tupac's 'Keep Your Head Up.' That track urged men to support women, and fathers to take responsibility to work with mothers in the raising of their children. Bashy's use of this chronotope, within the context of a valorisation of black boys (according to the video's subtitles, 'For black history month 2007'), represents a narrowing of the aspirations of both the Stairsteps' utopian and Tupac's somewhat more utilitarian performances.

Bashy's lyrics name a number of black males recognised within the grime scene, alongside others in the mainstream broadcast media. The video shows a number of young black men and boys, it celebrates the achievements of black artists, both male and female, and concludes with a roll call. The use of this form of genealogy and other mnemonic devices in constituting a community has been discussed by Walter Ong (2002: 46) in his work on oral cultures. Gilroy identifies that the form of citation that Kelly employs in 'Bump N Grind' through sampling 'does not play with the gap between then and now but rather uses it to assert a spurious continuity that adds legitimacy and gravity to the contemporary' (1994: 53). Alongside this creative ordering, Bashy's roll call produces a homeostatic society. The video constructs a form of social collectivity that, while not entirely excluding females, is principally concerned with fraternity. Its use of bright summer sun shining through leafy trees in the urban landscape represents this inner-city fraternity as 'positive,' and the long roll call has a prominent place in this representation. Rather than examining the representations of masculinity formed in the video more closely, I wish to place the issues outlined here alongside the more problematic clip, 'Bashy goin at Wiley and Scratchy (live).'

Bashy's rap in this clip begins: 'They said that my flow weren't good enough. Flow got good, said I weren't hood enough . . .' The lyrics are performed as a response to verbal attacks by Wiley and Roll Deep. These justifications for Bashy's response are followed by a declaration that he will now say what he feels, and then by a series of attacks, first against Wiley, and then Scratchy. The most problematic aspect of this attack may be Bashy's use of references to Wiley's sister, who he insults by calling her a slag, a hag, and comparing her to Wiley in drag. Following this, Bashy focusses his attention on Roll Deep before returning to Wiley, repeatedly attacking him through references to his sister. In a one minute and 15 second segment, Bashy lists a number of rappers and crews from across London that he will call on to perform various sex acts on Wiley's sister. This ends with the declaration that the entire grime 'industry' has 'been through' Wiley's sister and a question to the rival MC about how he feels about this.

The use of a roll call in both of these songs demonstrates the contrasting ways in which this rhetorical technique is used by rappers. The strategy itself is, of course, neither 'positive' or 'negative,' but is used to construct a notion of community, and simultaneously places the orator in a privileged position within that community. Bashy's rhetorical skills allow him to represent himself as possessing sufficient social capital to mobilise against Wiley. It is important to highlight his repeated assertions that he did not invite this conflict. The opening of his rap represents him as acting in defence of himself. This is followed by his playing the Dozens on Wiley and a movement from the defensive to the offensive. Bashy explicitly invokes and discards Wiley's mother as a means through which to stage his attack, in favour of his sister. Midway through the verbal assault Bashy pauses to call into question the status of his verbal play. The Dozens is clearly designed to attempt to produce a response from the opponent: 'The real aim of the dozen's was to get a dude so mad that he'd cry or get mad enough to fight' (Brown 1972: 206). Further to this, I suggest that it is important to consider how the playing of this game in contemporary London has both a regulating and reproductive social and economic role.

In a scene from Bashy's DVD, released after this verbal duel, the artist sits in a studio and acknowledges Wiley as 'one of the pioneers of grime,' before stating 'I do like him, me and him is cool now.' He then introduces a video recording of a conversation with Wiley in West London. The conversation between the two rappers turns around the issue of which is the superior artist. Both MCs refer to the age difference between Wiley and his younger rival. After Wiley states that Dizzee Rascal is the best artist and acknowledges that Bashy also is 'in the thing,' the scene is cut and we are briefly returned to Bashy's commentary in the studio. He now explains what the 'battle' was about, following which the street conversation is continued. Bashy, who holds the camera, now claims to have 'merked' Wiley. Wiley denies this and states 'whatever you say about my sister is air.' He goes on to argue: 'I'm not saying you merked me, I would never say that. What you did is, you woke me up because I was asleep to you. I was asleep to you if you understand. So you didn't merk me because merking means I'm never gonna come back and I'll walk off.' The DVD reveals how, in responding to put-downs from more recognised artists within this scene, Bashy sought to both defend his position and further develop his cultural capital in that field. Wiley's insistence that Bashy's references to his sister were 'air' foregrounds the ambivalent status of this play: simultaneously insubstantial nonsense and possessing a social force that can be brought to bear upon the ordering of the scene.

The conversation between the two artists engages with the nonsense talk of Bashy's verbal attack. Although Wiley dismisses anything said about his sister he admits being forced to respond to Bashy. This is not because some of the contents of Bashy's rap were regarded as justifiable. More importantly the Dozens game, as reformulated in this scene, requires a response in order to reproduce the social order through which Bashy launches his offensive. Seen from this perspective, Bashy refers to Wiley's sister as a synecdoche of Wiley himself, while also affirming the social ordering of young, black Londoners outside of the family structure. In order to maintain his position in this extrafamilial society Wiley needed to show that he was capable of defending himself/family members. There is a paradoxical affirmation of the family, but this is subordinated to the ability of the participants to respond within the rules of the game.

It is worth pausing for a moment to consider the historical development of the Dozens game within the black cultural tradition. Roger Abrahams highlights that the 'practice of mother-rhyming' has been observed in 'a number of groups in Africa, including the Yoruba, Efik, Dogon, and some Bantu tribes' (1972: 217). In relation to its use in the Caribbean, Abrahams connects it to the development of a masculine identity and rejection of family values. Through such play, boys learn how to develop a sense of self that is independent of their familial relations, while still acknowledging those relations. Abrahams argues that adolescent boys use the Dozens in the rejection of the 'feminine principle' (1993: 305), or mother figure, as part of the search for a masculinity outside the family home. The ultimate goal of the Dozens is the development of a form of self-possession that combines physical self-control with verbal facility. Afrikan Boy's recollection of 'destroying' one of his peers and his assertion that 'there was no such thing as who won or who lost, you just took away what you took away' identify an axis of ironic abuse that is ultimately affirming—if not of the individual, then of the social whole through which the subject develops a sense of self outside of the family unit.

It is also worth noting that Bashy's invective was directed to someone in a more senior age group, and a more recognised figure within the grime scene. Afrikan Boy's comments suggest that a sense of being above the game (while still participating in it) is crucial for the mastery that is necessary to withstand a verbal attack on one's self, while maintaining the ability to reply in a manner that is appreciated by the audience. Instead of prematurely attempting to class this practice as a form of misogyny, I suggest that the ritualised performance more likely has historical roots as a means of socialising Oedipal urges and producing healthier, extrafamilial, social relations. In considering the appropriation of the rap tradition in contemporary London, it is important to observe that the DVD, through which the 'battle' is explicated, and particular elements of the verbal duel—notably Wiley's response to 'Black Boys' in 'Off the Radar' on the *Race Against Time* album—contribute to the economic growth of the scene. Not only are the rhetorical skills developed through the Dozens game employed in more conventionally progressive tracks like 'Black Boys,' but artists working within the tradition have used the social order constitutive of the scene to economically develop what Bashy (in the DVD) terms the 'spitting industry.'

Although I have sought to highlight how the Dozens affirms the values of a wider community, I do not want to avoid the problematic gender politics at work within Bashy's songs. The playing of the game away from family space may partially explain why males figure disproportionally in his representation of the scene. However, the focus on black boys as a contribution to black history month substantially impoverishes the significance of black history. Even if his focus on the living is admitted—perhaps highlighting a concern with recent historical achievements of black MCs and media personalities—the marginalisation of females in his representation of black community indicates that his social and historical awareness are narrow, shortsighted, and politically regressive. This is more readily apparent when one considers the presence of females (both as rappers and active members of audiences) in the grime scene more generally. In my conversation with two girls on a bus, they both expressed an enjoyment of the lyrics of an artist called Specks—a friend of one of the girls' boyfriend. In the track they played to me, these girls highlighted the following line as being 'deep': 'If your mum comes out I'll move to your dad.' The song features Specks speaking to a (silent) female interlocutor, and plays on specific gender relations. Through this it represents Specks as willing to defy social conventions by challenging patriarchal authority. The girls' pleasure, derived from his verbal play on social norms, cannot be dismissed in the examination of the scene's gender politics. It is apparent that socially dominant constructions of femininity are not reinforced in the girls' appreciative response to this song. Through their participation in this scene they produce themselves as potential respondents to Specks's rhyming. They are able to both express pleasure at Specks's travesty of family values and inhabit a position capable of attacking (and therefore offering the possibility of reaffirming) the form of masculinity through which Specks constructs his persona. Bashy's 'Black Boys' does not entirely exclude women and girls from its roll call, but it fails to account for the far-reaching and complex contribution that they make to the history that he attempts to represent.

In this engagement with the lyrics of London's rap artists, it is not my intention to offer a simple opposition of Roots Manuva to Bashy, as good and bad artists. There are substantial differences between them that would make such an opposition untenable. These include their difference of age, the relation between this and their participation in distinct rap scenes, and the generic expectations of the UK hip-hop and grime scenes. However, there are more particular differences between the two artists that can only be ascertained through attentiveness to their work. Roots Manuva's lyrics reveal a concern with reinvesting a profane art form with an embodied techno-spirituality. He presents himself as a shamanic figure, and his performance of 'Witness' and other songs forms part of his organisation of the consciousness of his audience along particular ethical-political lines.

Nevertheless, Roots Manuva uses many of the same cultural resources as Bashy. Bashy's uses of the roll call demonstrates that his development as an artist has involved taking both 'negative' and (within the limited terms of black male uplift) socially 'progressive' positions. Although Roots Manuva's 'Witness' may be more inventive than the examples of Bashy's work that I have discussed, the literary value of these lyrics is not my central concern here. Rather than opposing these artists to one another, I have sought to present contrasting forms of analysis. I suggest that they may be used alongside one another to offer a more fully developed examination of London's contemporary black culture than either technique could deliver alone. I will now attend to the representation of gender and gender politics in two specific works, before broadening my consideration of black cultural politics.

GENDERED REPRESENTATIONS OF BLACK LONDONERS

In the opening of 'Unorthodox Daughter' No. Lay sends shout-outs to several artists. Through this rhetorical form she acknowledges these artists and expresses her affiliation with a particular group within the grime scene. This is preceded, in the accompanying video, with a series of shots of a council estate, each from a different perspective. No. Lay first appears sitting with another young woman, watching TV, while a child jumps in the foreground. A male artist's track plays during this opening segment, and it is his video that we see on the TV in several other shots. No. Lay is then shown walking through a corridor, leaving the flat, and we hear the shout-outs as the door shuts behind her. The scene changes to her performing in a bedroom studio as two young men sit listening to her perform. Her rap opens with an attack on unspecified others that is comparable to Bashy's more focussed assault on particular individuals. The agonistic assertion of herself takes the form of a verbal strike against the inauthenticity of other (male) MCs, as well as posing females. The substance of No. Lay's authenticity is expressed through the image of herself as a 'chick' whose rapping is sufficiently potent to hospitalise those who are mere pretenders. Like Bashy, No. Lay's opening establishes her authenticity and lyrical ability as a rapper. Whereas he presented his playing of the Dozens on Wiley as a response to attacks on his flow and claims that he was neither 'hood' nor 'real,' No. Lay preemptively establishes herself as a potent female MC who is able to take on any frauds, male or female.

Her verse continues through an attack on 'looser' chicks, with a warning of the sexually transmitted diseases that can be caught as a result of such behaviour. She then refers to the violence of the illicit drug trade, girls who bitch, boys who act as police informants, and a variety of other social tensions. The verse ends with a warning about the consequences of inauthenticity, through the depiction of social isolation in prison, coupled with sexual betrayal and broken friendships. During the chorus the video predominantly shows No. Lay in the foreground with a number of young men, either behind or around her. The images emphasise the importance of others' support, which is thematised towards the end of the verse. They also function in the representation of 'truth' as social solidarity and personal authenticity. During the second verse, in which No. Lay emphasises social solidarity, the supremacy of her linguistic abilities, and rap music as a means of making money, the video continues to rapidly shift perspectives, accentuating the speed of No. Lay's delivery. In addition to the views of her walking or driving around the estate with her crew or with a small group of young, black women, several shots show her inside a flat, with the girl seen in the opening sequence braiding No. Lay's hair as she in turn plaits the child's.

Throughout the track No. Lay attacks the use of guns in rap lyrics and in life. Further to this, she uses the hyperbole of other 'fake' artists, and their talk of gunplay, against which to construct her authenticity. Her criticism of divisive and inauthentic girls contrasts with her representation of herself caring for a child and being cared for by another girl. These contrasting strategies establish No. Lay as real. This representation of authentic black femininity is articulated with the redemptive power of rap and working-class solidarity. In addition to referring to the cathartic power of the form and its potential to lead to economic gain, in the final verse her tight lyrics and authenticity are contrasted with the loose talk and behaviour of others. Looseness, individualism, and fakeness are associated with a variety of social ills, from sexually transmitted diseases to being killed. She represents a black authenticity that is composed of social solidarity, vernacular articulacy, and the need to deal with the difficulties of poverty and other challenges by toughening up.

Like 'Unorthodox Daughter,' Dizzee Rascal's 'Sirens' deals with issues of poverty, gender, and the urban environment. There is a significant gap between the video and lyrics, so I wish to treat them separately before engaging with that disjuncture. The video opens with images of a housing estate. A horn and hounds are heard before the instrumental begins, and are followed by a proleptic scene of the video's climax: Dizzee trapped by dogs. As the first verse begins, he is seen at home rapping with a younger boy. A photograph of an older man wearing a trilby stands between them, representing the historical contiguity of this black cultural form. This domestic scene is disrupted by the violent entry of a huntsman. Following his break in to their home we see a modernist painting of a face—half black, half white. As the horseman proceeds into the living room, he smashes objects out of his way, and the horse steps on the framed representation of the older man. The cracked glass symbolises the death of this figure of paternity and black cultural tradition. Before the huntsman is able to discover the younger boy, Dizzee dons a fur-lined coat, steps in front of the painting, and calls to the hunter, drawing him away from his sibling. As the horseman begins his pursuit, we see him emerge from behind a wall, upon which is mounted an African face carving. The juxtaposition of the white man dressed in his red hunting jacket and the carving develops the imagery in the painting and the video's theme of race and class.

This theme is further developed through a number of written signs, including a poster that asks 'Drowning in debt?' and graffiti declaring 'Only cowards steal from the poor.' The horseman's horn is sonically juxtaposed with the sirens of the instrumental, producing an association between racist policing, hunting, and class conflict. Horsemen are seen smashing recreational facilities on the Orgreave Estate as they pursue the young black man. The reference to the Battle of Orgreave and the miners' strikes of the 1980s further reinforces the articulation of race and class in the video. When Dizzee knocks on a window to seek refuge, a white woman is shown closing the curtains and moving away. This injects into the dominant theme of race and class a gender politics that positions white women as (at the least) unconcerned with the plight of working-class, black males. However, the grinning faces of the female hunters intensify this disjuncture between white women and black men. After being caught Dizzee removes his coat, exposing his body. As he does so, several huntresses look on intensely, with voyeuristic grins. The face of one of these women is smeared with the blood of the catch, as part of an initiation, by an older huntsman. The initiation practice and the representation of the black male as an object of the white female gaze complicate the representation of race that is figured in the modernist painting at the beginning of the video. White women in the dominated and dominating classes are depicted, on the one hand, as unconcerned with the plight of black men, and on the other, with an intense and lethal interest through which white females may enter into the socially dominant culture. Black women are entirely absent from the video. This omission suggests, as a corollary to the brutalisation of working-class blacks by the dominant social group, the suppression of the interests and identities of black females within the representation of the subordinated race.

The lyrics of 'Sirens' tell the story of the arrest of the rapper by the police, following the assault of a man and woman by him and his friend. The second verse is framed by the statement 'let's go back to that old-school story telling shit.' Aside from this the song offers no other justification for its narrative and closes with a defiant declaration: 'I'll break the law, I will never change.' The first verse is composed of four quatrains, and relates the arrest of the rapper and his response to being told of the evidence that the police have of his acts: 'Gotta stay calm gotta keep my cool/ If I go jail I'll be a damn fool/ Gotta rise up gotta stand up tall/ Can't let them see the end of Dizzee Rascal.' The second verse has a much faster pace, is composed of rhyming couplets, and describes the boys' stalking of their victims, the attack, and their flight from the scene:

> . . .
> We was on a robbing spree, I forgot to mention Clayton
> Was this bredder rolling with us, he was scared and it was blatant

> He was prang but back to the story, Adar spotted a man
> Straight ahead of us in the distance with his wifey holding hands
> So we followed them through this little alleyway into the flats
> When we thought the time was perfect, we crept up and we attacked
> I took the first swing, unexpected causing panic
> We was ruthless causing agony in public, it was tragic
> Me and Adar lost the plot, acting like we was from Hell
> Beat this bredder to the floor, moved his wifey up as well
> Clayton stood back shaking, wishing that he'd never came
> Then from out of nowhere was Alicia screaming out my name.
>   . . .

The horrific narrative depicts the rapper and his accomplice violently assaulting a man and woman. It also shows Clayton's fear and revulsion at Dizzee and Adar's actions, thus foregrounding the brutality of the attack. In reciting the rap, I find the linguistic control necessary to deliver this verse within the tempo of the soundtrack to be substantial. There is a tension between that control and the statement that the rapper 'lost the plot.' Indeed, the references to perfectly timing one's 'attack' and the 'shit' that is difficult to 'digest' are appropriate characterisations of the verse's form and theme. Although the final verse slows from the considerably rapid pace of the second, the rapper's unrepentant stance persists:

> It's no joke, man, woman, and child I'm seeking
> See, no sex, no age, I'm creeping
> Anything for the dough, code of the wheelers
> Duck from the Feds and I roll with the dealers
> Par with the hard heads and young offenders
> No, my life ain't nothing like Eastenders

Despite the earlier reference to storytelling, the final verse implies a verisimilitude. I argue that the rap maintains a claim to truth that lies in the story's form as much as its theme. The pace of Dizzee's performance is rapid—not frenzied. His control over this material, combined with the rap's unrepentant narrative, is a significant quality of 'Sirens.' The song sets the shameless assault within the form of a tragic representation of social tumult. This tragedy does not allow any easy way of finding redemption, but presents itself without justification. The tragic rap employs a form of aesthetic nihilism, and Dizzee Rascal's unrepentant representation of a street robbery challenges his audience to engage with the complexity of his form of representation.

By narrating the story from the perspective of the attacker, listeners are denied the privileged position from which to view the story that is available to viewers of the video. The rapper affirms his association with 'dealers,' 'hard heads,' and 'young offenders' and speaks to the listener from that social position, with considerable linguistic control, rhetorical force, and (while avoiding any glamorisation of the attack) substantial sagacity.

Whereas the video places the rapper in the bleak context of urban poverty, destruction of public provision for social recreation, and the policing of blacks by a hostile, white society, the song speaks from, and asserts the integrity of, the position of someone subject to these forces, but without reference to them. The video represents this tragedy not only through the blooding of the young huntress, but also in the image of the roundabout 'hazard' sign with which it begins. This indicates that what we see is part of an ongoing cycle. 'Sirens' also compares the rapper's stalking of the couple with fox hunting and the policing of young black men, as rituals of violence through an understated, 'hard-boiled' aesthetic (Ellison 1995: 36–37). In doing so, the video's soundtrack complicates the attempt to take the privileged position that is constructed through its images.

The rapped lyrics and video are composed through an aesthetic nihilism. It is necessary to distinguish this from the notion of meaninglessness and hopelessness that Cornel West asserts 'increasingly pervades black communities' (1993: 22). Through an aesthetic nihilism—that is, artistic composition through discarded or deprecated material—black Londoners may in fact *affirm* themselves by drawing upon and engaging with the conditions in which they live. The gritty representation of the assault in the rap should also be seen in the context of the development of the grime genre itself. By turning the word 'grime' into the appreciative term 'grimy' and privileging it as an aesthetic quality, young Londoners identified and recuperated the undervalued, soiled, and undesirable in the urban environment and brought it into the world of music. This process developed through the production of soundscapes that articulated ideas of urban life with feelings of coldness, as in Wiley's 'Eski beat,' or the idea of filth captured in the word that came to identify the scene in its entirety. The affirmation of social relations with the groups referred to in the final verse presents the issue of how to deal with a social whole that includes those who, being subject to the dehumanising forces depicted in the video, act in the inhuman manner enunciated in the lyrics. That this issue is represented through a tragic plot underscores the difficulty of resolving it through existing social and economic relations. 'Sirens' punctuates the urgency of producing an art that is capable of representing the marginalised and undervalued while presenting itself without shame.

Richard Wright's discussion of *Native Son* can be usefully brought to bear upon the problematic presented by 'Sirens.' In his comments on the dehumanising effects of racism, Wright is critical of superficial efforts to distract black boys by liberal whites. He draws attention to the role of these efforts in preserving social and economic inequality. His essay, 'How "Bigger" was Born,' describes the issues that confronted him in trying to construct this character. Detailing how he approached the composition of Bigger's 'dual' social consciousness, Wright states:

> I placed the nationalistic side first, not because I agreed with Bigger's wild and intense hatred of white people, but because his hate had placed

him, like a wild animal at bay, in a position where he was most symbolic and explainable. In other words, his nationalist complex was for
me a concept through which I could grasp more of the total meaning
of his life than I could in any other way. I tried to approach Bigger's
snarled and confused nationalist feelings with conscious and informed
ones of my own. Yet, Bigger was not nationalist enough to feel the need
of religion or the folk culture of his own people. What made Bigger's
social consciousness most complex was the fact that he was hovering
unwanted between two worlds—between powerful America and his
own stunted place in life—and I took upon myself the task of trying to
make the reader feel this No Man's Land. The most that I could say of
Bigger was that he felt the need for a whole life and acted out of that
need; that was all.

(Wright 1989: xxiv)

After spending a considerable time contemplating this character, Wright
pinpoints two specific events that committed him to the task of writing
Bigger's story. The first of these was his work in a boy's club—'an institution which tried to reclaim the thousands of Negro Bigger Thomases from
the dives and the alleys of the Black Belt.' Through this institution wealthy
whites provided a diversion for the deprived black boys of the city in an
attempt to ensure that they 'might not roam the streets and harm the valuable white property which adjoined the Black Belt' (Wright 1989: xxvii).
A further event is of more direct significance to the complex set of problems
presented by 'Sirens':

The second event that spurred me to write of Bigger was more personal
and subtle. I had written a book of short stories which was published
under the title of *Uncle Tom's Children*. When the reviews of that book
began to appear, I realized that I had made an awfully naive mistake.
I found that I had written a book which even bankers' daughters could
read and weep over and feel good about. I swore to myself that if I ever
wrote another book, no one would weep over it; that it would be so
hard and deep that they would have to face it without the consolation
of tears. It was this that made me get to work in dead earnest.

What I have termed an aesthetic nihilism, in contemporary rap music,
challenges the audience to respond 'without the consolation of tears.'
The unrepentant representation of the subject position of a contemporary
black-English Bigger confronts listeners with the complex economic, social,
and psychological forces that produce dangerously alienated youths and
social misery.

Both Dizzee Rascal and No. Lay engage with issues of working-class solidarity, the urban environment, and racialised identities. In the videos that
I have analysed here, the artists also represent the gendered reproduction of

black culture. The intergenerational hair-plaiting in 'Unorthodox Daughter' parallels the rapping in a circle in 'Sirens.' Proceeding from these artists' engagement with the maintenance of the social individual's integrity, I wish to distinguish these representations of the black self from globalised, American images of blackness, before broadening my consideration of black cultural politics in London's rap scenes.

As I write this chapter Rihanna is currently promoting her album, *Rated R*, prior to her tour of the UK. The video to the song 'Hard,' which features Young Jeezy's rap lyrics, shows Rihanna in a variety of militarised settings. She rapturously fires an automatic weapon, and confidently struts through the desert in a black spiked jacket (figuring a transformation of her breasts into protective armour) while bombs explode in the sand around her. Here, US hip-hop works at the service of the state in its drive to gain support for its efforts in the 'war on terror.' The 'hard' femininity represented by her riding the gun barrel of a pink tank is one that sexualises war. It positions itself in opposition to an Islamic other, which is depicted through the Arabic graffiti on the side of a building as Rihanna sings, 'who'd think they'd test me now, run through your town I'll shut it down.' In his discussion of the aestheticisation of politics Benjamin quotes Marinetti's manifesto on the Italian colonial war against Ethiopia: 'War is beautiful because it initiates the dreamt-of metalization of the human body' (2007: 241). Benjamin's critique opposes the politicisation of art to fascist aesthetics in which mankind's 'self alienation has reached such a degree that it can experience its own destruction as an aesthetic experience of the first order' (Benjamin 2007: 242). Rihanna's video is only one of the more recent products in the process of the cooptation and globalisation of African-American culture by corporate interests and of a state that maintains the mass imprisonment and economic marginalisation of blacks. In that process, artists such as Rihanna offer African-Americans compensatory stardom, global prestige, and a platform for aesthetic expression. I draw attention to Rihanna's track here in order to highlight the necessity of nuanced analysis that avoids assumptions of resistance and marginality in black cultural products. In contrast to 'Hard,' both No. Lay and Dizzee offer their audiences significantly different routes through which to deal with social injustice, economic exploitation, and the construction of oppositional, gendered identities. Their representations can be seen to either resist the state or to figure dominant representations of English identity as an active part of the subordination of working-class blacks and a fractured social world.

RAP AND POSTCOLONIAL LONDON'S CULTURAL POLITICS

In the final section of this chapter I will broaden my analysis of black cultural politics in contemporary London. In order to more fully investigate rap's role in that politics it is necessary to alter the focus. Consequently

I will address the processes through which rappers develop their awareness of the world they inhabit and their social critiques of that world. No. Lay's lyrics refer to the cathartic power of rap as a means of dealing with the challenges of urban dwelling. This should be considered along with the way that Bashy's playing of the Dozens demonstrates how practices that deal with Oedipal urges have been organised into a means of developing wider social recognition and economic gain. These artists' representations highlight the need for an examination of MCs' engagements with contemporary life in the city.

The grime scene's exploration of themes of violence connected with mainstream media debates in 2008 on 'London teen killings.'[1] A number of MCs and DJs linked this issue to questions about the policing of young people. They also expressed concerns with the role of art in dealing with social violence. In the first track that I want to discuss, in relation to how London's black public sphere responded to this issue, Sincere challenges the government's failure to act to protect young people from violence: 'Its a god damn shame Gordon Brown don't care/ Cause all I hear is gun shots and see fiends around here.' Some time after the track began to be heard on radio sets around London, the prime minister announced plans to tackle what the government termed 'Youth Crime.'[2] However, those announcements (such as having offenders go to hospitals to witness the injuries caused by knives)[3] were met with confusion, and the plans were reported in the mainstream media as inadequate and out of touch. Furthermore, despite the subsequent identification of several of the alleged murderers of London's teenagers as adults (including one 45-year-old civil servant), the government failed to acknowledge any connection between these killings and wider social issues. Instead it remained actively complicit in the pathologisation of urban youth. It is also worth noting that these events took place in a context in which the Labour government had effected a massive redistribution of wealth to prop up the banking system and Gordon Brown had failed to make any announcement on his race relations policy.

Rather than looking to the state to solve a problem that it was implicated in producing, Sincere's rap offers a critique of socially harmful ways of making money, and connects this with urban violence. It adopts this critical position while also presenting itself as a legitimate alternative means of economic gain. The track deals with violence amongst youths and racist policing practices that are employed in the maintenance of social inequality. Further to this, it attempts to represent a black-English culture that is capable of independently transforming the economic position of the groups that it simultaneously conserves socially.

Rap's role in reproducing the social relations through which London's vernacular culture is developed can be observed as the video opens with an image of a fish and chip shop. The store sign advertises both 'pies and cod' and 'curry sauce,' in a reference to the syncretic development of black-English cultural identity. The video represents a vernacular postcoloniality. Its attempt to recuperate an identity that is inclusive of nonwhites by constructing a vernacular Englishness goes further than adopting the relative openness of British cultural identity (MacCabe et al. 2006: 35–36). A group of young, black and white men and women stand outside purchasing the 'good fast food' from the salesperson. Almost in direct opposition to media stories of the menace that 'hoodies'[4] pose to society, Sincere initially appears with his face covered by a hood, before taking it down. The shift of scenes in Sincere's video—from the street, through a musical stage, to a brightly lit set with 'Sincere' in lights—traces an attempt to represent rap as a legitimate means of escaping urban poverty without calling upon the state for assistance. This representation of the aspiration of economic progress is coupled with the expression of lost social and political unity and the rapper's statement that his efforts are directed towards restoring it. Sincere attempts to affirm a black-English, socioeconomic, and cultural development that is inclusive of the working-class whites represented in the video. It is significant that economic gain is foregrounded in the track's attempt to represent a vernacular black-English citizenship. Whereas No. Lay refers to poverty as a source of the social tensions she describes, economic uplift is represented in 'Once Upon A Time' as a key to overcoming social barriers and gaining entry to the life of the nation.

In the media context in which this track was produced and circulated, Doytun Adebayo's comments on rap music fed into a cycle of newspaper reports connecting black youths and rap music with violent criminality. The simplistic assertion, in *The Sun*, that after '12 hours of gangsta rap I could have knifed someone'[5] suggests that young people naïvely ingest stories that contain violence, and then act that violence out. This overlooks both the constructive artistic engagements with social violence that artists such as No. Lay and Sincere attempt and the more probing representation of street violence that Dizzee advances. Adebayo's understanding of rap and its connection to London's social structures falls far below the level of sophistication demanded by the work of these MCs. Rather than shying away from violence in their lyrics, these rappers foreground a political commitment against violence and racism. The suppression of this aspect of grime culture in the mainstream media in favour of facile scare stories clearly hampers the efforts of these artists.

In contrast to Sincere's song, which directly critiques the government and racist policing in his representation of the need for unity, Afrikan Boy's 'Lidl' employs a rather more ludic strategy in its representation of black urban life. The first and second verses describe the rapper being caught shop-lifting. After he is banned from Lidl and Asda supermarkets in these verses, the third deals with the issue of immigration. Although Afrikan Boy states that the first two verses are based on his direct personal experience as a schoolboy, the third also drew upon his proximity to actual events. The track deals with all these matters in a humorous manner: 'I take a serious issue and then rap about it in this sort of . . . comical way.' He recalls that seeing people organising others' entry into the country was an ordinary matter. However, he employs a comic mode in order that his audience can enjoy the humorous aspect while also hearing the more serious issues in his work: 'It's everyday life. I hear my mum talking on the phone like "ah, how am I gonna get this person in?" . . . Its everyday life, so I just put it there for—you know—as a joke, but . . . there's truth behind the joke.' The progress of the 'smelly' breathed rapper, from being thrown out of the supermarket by a Nigerian security guard to having an immigration officer knock on his door, highlights links between black urban poverty and global economic inequalities. The comic justification for his attempted theft—'EMA didn't pay me'—highlights the poverty of working-class, urban youth dependent upon this support.[6] It also alludes to the difficulties that marginalised groups face in negotiating a course through the social service and education systems.

In a discussion of the various interpretations of this song offered to him by listeners, he points out one that he considered particularly interesting: 'Afrikan Boy is this kid yeah. And he's so broke that he has to shoplift in the poorest . . . shop.' Although he emphasises that he based 'Lidl' on his personal experience, his engagement with his audience following its composition is part of his sociopolitical and artistic development. His comments about others' interpretations of his work highlight the social processes through which meanings are produced in this culture. This is perhaps even more significant in relation to this track, as Afrikan Boy did not make the decision to publish the song. It was placed on the Internet by someone in the studio. Nevertheless, the track forms a significant part of his performances, and his audiences respond to it with energetic dancing and antiphonic chanting.

In order to put this track in its legal and political context, it is necessary to draw attention to the coming to an end of the rioting of 300 African migrants in Italy.[7] The immediate cause for the rioting was the shooting of several migrant farm workers by Italian youths. This may be compared to the shooting of ethnic minorities in Sweden. Between December 2009 and October 2010 Peter Mangs, a Swedish national, carried out at more than a dozen gun attacks against members of Malmö's large immigrant community. Although Britain may currently tend to employ more Polish migrants as farm labourers than Africans, the electoral fortunes of the BNP during the first decade of the new millennium and Anders Behring Breivik's murderous campaign against multiculturalism highlight the rising impact of racism across Britain and Europe. It is clear that Afrikan Boy's particular local experience is connected to broader legal and political structures. Although he does not highlight these specific structures himself, he insists that his lyrics deal with 'a serious, deep issue.'

Afrikan Boy's emphasis on personal experience is a significant feature of his cultural production. His comic mode of representation in 'Lidl' contrasts with the formal construction of 'Kunta Kinte.' Nevertheless, he insists that 'what the track means to me is just to be myself.' However, the track's use of sampled audio from the film *Roots*, depicting racist brutality, foregrounds conditions in which being oneself is extremely difficult—if not deadly. His personalisation of this meaning suggests his awareness and openness to the making of other meanings by his audiences. Afrikan Boy identifies additional sociohistorical concerns in his discussion of the lyrics' relation to the Tribal House beat that they were written for: 'The type of music which is big in London now, I wanted to link it back to its original roots, cause obviously Tribal House music, it comes from African music. . . . Imagine if I took that track . . . back to the deep roots of Africa so they could then use it as a tribal ritual or something.' As part of his performance of this song Afrikan Boy builds in an element of spontaneity, with a 'freestyle' at the end in which he repeats: 'You can take my . . . ,' inserting various references as they occur to him. These may include trainers, clothes, or body parts. The construction of the song as part of a ritual that connects his London audience to Africa, while dealing with contemporary issues, bears some similarity to Rodney Smith's shamanic performance of the Roots Manuva persona. Both artists engage in a socially active process with their audiences through which they articulate 'distinct "moments" of knowing' (Taussig 1987: 463). Although Afrikan Boy does not attack political figures in Sincere's direct manner, his organisation of the audience in the form of a tribal community with a black historical consciousness is an important part of the development of London's black public sphere. The use of humour does not detract from the seriousness of the issues that he raises, but facilitates the effective delivery of the song's underlying themes. His concern with racism and poverty does not advance an economic solution. Instead he questions the construction of identity through possession of branded goods: 'My name is Kunta Kinte, I don't drive a Hummer, but I get many whips from my old slave master.' His lyrics invoke the social memory of slavery and allow members of his audience to make new meanings and construct new relations to the continuing historical effects of racism.

CONCLUSION

I want to conclude this chapter by recalling the complex issues represented and circulated in London's black public sphere. These representations are motivated by the pursuit of economic justice, as well as the desire to bring about more just social relations. The challenge they present to their audience draws on the memory of racial terror, and attempts to produce an affirmative collectivity through the recuperation of the discarded and undervalued. Dizzee Rascal's 'Sirens' troubles the position of the viewer. At the video's climax the camera's frame is identified with the white female gaze. However, despite witnessing the initiation of the white woman into the dominant culture, the viewer is denied the spectacle of the sacrificed black male. This elision is clearly related to the limits of what mainstream society is prepared to accept within a music video. Nevertheless, the rap lyrics present us with the brutal assault of a man and woman by two black boys. The rap lyrics and music video explore the politics of representation, as well as the experience of dwelling in the margins of urban life. 'Sirens' demands from its audience a far more sophisticated response than the sort that Adebayo is willing to trade in. However, my examination of its lyrics is not intended to diminish the significance of embodied interpretations produced through the dance scene. It is also necessary to challenge postcolonial scholars' comfortable habituation within literary studies. Disinterested, contemplative discussion of rap lyrics will remain impoverished without engagement with the sites and processes of performance. It is necessary to begin work in earnest on methodological tools that can help to provide a fuller account of the social and aesthetic significance of black popular culture.

The study of these cultural products and spaces can help us to develop our understanding of the formation of subaltern identities. The means through which rap songs are produced and circulated draws attention to the role of technology in shaping the consciousness of contemporary youth. The forms of social solidarity constructed through oppositional representations, such as those produced by Afrikan Boy, No. Lay, and Dizzee Rascal, cannot be overlooked in discussions of race, gender, and class, or in studies of youth subcultures. Their gendered representations foreground the economic conditions that are faced by working-class blacks in London and connect the importance of social solidarity to overcoming urban poverty. Roots Manuva, No. Lay, and Sincere all emphasise an economic interest in rapping and attach this interest to producing forms of collective well-being. Along with Bashy, their work highlights how the black cultural tradition is appropriated in postcolonial London and adapted to deal with contemporary social and economic needs. The strategies employed by these rappers perform a variety of social functions: from the commemoration of slavery to the material affirmation of social being. The circulation of their songs and music videos makes significant contributions to the political economy of London's black public sphere.

NOTES

1. http://news.bbc.co.uk/1/hi/uk/7395875.stm [Date Accessed 5 January 2010].
2. http://news.bbc.co.uk/1/hi/uk/7777963.stm [Date Accessed 11 September 2010].
3. http://news.bbc.co.uk/1/hi/uk_politics/7503845.stm [Date Accessed 11 September 2010].
4. http://news.bbc.co.uk/1/hi/england/beds/bucks/herts/4365542.stm [Date Accessed 3 July 2013].
5. http://www.thesun.co.uk/sol/homepage/news/justice/1519825/After-12-hours-of-gangsta-rap-I-could-have-knifed-someone.html [Date Accessed 7 January 2010].
6. The education maintenance allowance is provided to those who want to continue their education after school-leaving age. The scheme was abolished in

England by the Conservative and Liberal Democrat coalition government. However, Afrikan Boy's 'Lidl' was produced and released prior to the 2010 election that brought the coalition to power.

7. http://news.bbc.co.uk/1/hi/world/europe/8447990.stm [Date Accessed 30 January 2010].

5   From a 'Junior Spesh' to the 'Keys to the Bentley'
The Routes of Grimey London

London's rap artists distinguish themselves from and position themselves in relation to other artists, through their creative work. The collective activities of MCs and DJs contribute to the organisation of distinct scenes within the city's cultural field. Dizzee Rascal's collaboration with Calvin Harris on 'Dance Wiv Me' and his release of the 1970s dance-influenced 'Dirty Disco' distinguished him from other grime MCs, as well as from his earlier creative work. Such releases are part of a process through which this once marginalised scene develops its mainstream audience. Through this process grime artists modify their relation to other social scenes and explore grime's potential for economic growth. Dizzee's shift from the formal and thematic qualities of *Boy in the Corner* to attract a mainstream audience was criticised by an emerging artist, who preferred the 'tuggy' style of the earlier album to what he saw as more recent, 'manufactured' offerings. Dizzee's appearance on the BBC 1 programme, *Friday Night with Jonathan Ross*, in April 2010 revealed his awareness of such critiques: 'I'm called a sellout every day, but it's progress, it's progress.' Dizzee's comment indicates his trajectory through Britain's cultural field. It also demonstrates the tensions that operate between formal innovation, notions of authenticity, economic growth, and proximity to the social world in which one's skills as a rapper are developed.

All of these factors have some bearing upon rap artists and their work. Those factors also inform audience members' perspectives of the scenes in which they too are active agents. In Bourdieu's formulation of the field of cultural production, he specifies that

> authors only exist and subsist under the structured constraints of the field (e.g. the objective relations that are established between genres). They affirm the differential deviation which constitutes their position, their point of view—understood as the perspective from a given point in the field—by assuming, actually or virtually, one of the possible aesthetic positions in the field (and thus assuming a position in relation to other positions).
>
> (1993: 184)

Dizzee's interview with Jonathan Ross is indicative of his participation in the mainstreaming of London's black culture. Bourdieu's analysis of the French literary field is relevant to the oppositions constructed through attempts to attract a mainstream British and international audience, as well as accusations of 'selling out' from the values embedded in a more localised, 'tuggy' style. He highlights that the relative autonomy of the cultural sphere does not make this field completely independent of other spheres in the social whole:

> Thus, the power relationships between the 'conservatives' and 'innovators', the orthodox and heretical, the old and the new, are greatly dependent on the state of external struggles and on the reinforcement that one or another may find from without—for example, for the heretical, in the emergence of new clienteles, whose appearance is often linked to changes in the educational system.
>
> (Bourdieu 1993: 184–185)

In popular British culture, rap is closely connected to working-class and ethnic minority groups. The stakes that are involved in the struggle within the cultural field are closely related to external factors and political interests. These include the support of one's social group, as well as the possibilities of acquiring economic wealth. Bourdieu emphasises that his theory of the field does not entail a mechanistic determinism, stressing:

> [A]gents, writers, artists, intellectuals construct their own creative project according, first of all, to their perception of the available possibilities afforded by the categories of perception and appreciation inscribed in their habitus through a certain trajectory and, secondly, to their predisposition to take advantage of or reject those possibilities in accordance with interests associated with their position in the game.
>
> (Bourdieu 1993: 184)

This principle can be used to inform understanding of how MCs and DJs' artistic work reveals their own position and dispositions. It is also useful in mapping the forces that act upon the city's rap scenes.

Recalling the artists that he admires, Seeker identifies Estelle, Klashnekoff, MFD, Cashmere, and H2O. He goes on to state that there are other artists that he is aware of, but that 'they tend to be more on that grime scene . . . or the music that they write doesn't appeal to me.' As a result of his identification of himself through his interest in UK hip-hop, Seeker represents his cultural field by positioning artists that he admires within that scene. He then distances UK hip-hop as a whole from the grime scene. For commercial considerations this distinction may be untenable, and a senior record company executive informed me that as far as he was concerned the two scenes had merged. Nevertheless, like other artists and listeners I interviewed, Seeker distinguished between the two scenes even while demonstrating his awareness of artists who incorporate a variety of styles into their repertoire. As one example, he highlighted that Klashnekoff had released a track with 'grime elements.' In positioning himself within UK hip-hop, he associated artists such as Lethal Bizzle, Dizzee Rascal, Kano, and Wiley with music that thematised violence and other 'negative elements.' As a corollary to this, grime music was identified by him with such themes, as well as with an aesthetic that includes a relatively high tempo and distinct 'sound.'

Seeker's acknowledgement of the complexity of representing the different scenes and the artists that operate within them also led him to raise a further layer of complexity involved in the use of music by audiences:

> I listen to a lot of music that is not of the most positive element . . . so you have American artists like Mobb Deep who talk about beef and war in the most grimiest way. You know the type of things that they go through or the life that they live. And I can listen to it and not be influenced by it. But I can appreciate the creativity that has gone into the production and also the way that they use to describe certain elements in society in a metaphorical way. So how I'm able to listen to that negative element and flip it into a positive I think is something that very few seem to be able to do—or want to do, because everyone can do it. But then its a case of right, do you then now look at that lifestyle and try to imitate it . . . or do you look at it and see if you can flip it into a positive element in what you're doing.

Further to identifying a creativity in the aesthetic nihilism of these artists' work, Seeker's comments indicate the development of a sophisticated audience in parts of the scene with which he identifies. Through this he distinguishes himself as a privileged interpreter within the field and indicates some of the skills that are involved in making the forms of judgements his position requires.

Despite his demonstration of sophisticated interpretative skills, Seeker's representation of himself as a 'conscious' rapper within the UK hip-hop scene obscures the significance of grime's formal and thematic qualities. This is indicative of the disposition that he has developed through his investments in that social space. The profession of some grime artists of their ignorance of US hip-hop until late in their cultural development distances their scene from hip-hop in a way that Seeker, and UK hip-hop artists in general, cannot. Furthermore, grime's relations to garage, and through that to jungle and earlier forms of British rap music, identify the genre as a post-hip-hop, sociocultural development. Significantly, this youth subculture flourished during a period of stagnation in the UK hip-hop scene. The decline and stagnation of UK hip-hop is suggestive of a cultural politics from which grime, with its emphasis on local particularity, has benefited.

In Bourdieu's concern with the French peasantry and the limited options available to them to preserve their identity through the representation of their social world, he specifically denies them the possibility of 'the "black is beautiful" strategy' (Bourdieu 1984: 384). It is clear from this that his interpretative frame acknowledges the cultural politics employed by African-Americans to challenge their social and political marginalisation. It is equally clear that the analysis of contemporary rap music must move beyond the limits imposed by the specific conditions that focussed Bourdieu's analysis. By contesting (or even ignoring) American hip-hop artists, grime MCs valorise their own work and aesthetically distinct cultural space.[1] Grime artists position themselves as inheritors of jungle by employing their rapid tempo and developing a local audience for their cultural production. Seeker highlights the connection that he sees between the aesthetic and the social. But his distance from those American artists makes his strategy of contemplative inversion easier than with tracks such as Dizzee's 'I Luv U,' which presents a troubling image of male/female gender relations in London. Seeker's willingness to engage with the complexities that artists such as Mobb Deep present, but not with those of Dizzee Rascal, who is much closer socially, suggests another issue concerning the interpretative practices of agents in the city's rap scenes. His comments do not address the challenge of coming to terms with the social, political, and economic conditions that artists and their communities find themselves in. Nor do they probe the relation between these conditions and the cultural production of those who dwell in them.

Ty is critical of grime artists from another perspective. In his discussion of the position of British hip-hop artists, he states:

> We're treated like boys. If I come with a new record and I go to Radio 1, the same box I'm in is the same box Tynchy Stryder is in, the same box Dizzee Rascal's in, the same box Kano is in. But we don't make the same music. But that's how they view us. We're just a bunch of black boys trying to get on their play list. That's it.

His desire to be treated differently to grime artists connects aesthetic distinctions with the age difference between him and London's younger generation of rap artists. This distinction between positions within the field of cultural production is the opposite side of Ty's recognition that he does not possess the same standing as 'a doctor or a lawyer' in the wider society. Through oppositions such as these, artists attempt to construct their position within the cultural field. Bourdieu states,

> the invention of the writer, in the modern sense of the term, is inseparable from the progressive invention of a particular social game, which I term the *literary field* and which is constituted as it establishes its autonomy, that is to say, its specific laws of functioning, within the field of power.
> (Bourdieu 1993: 163, emphasis in text)

It is necessary to bear in mind that to understand these social individuals is first of all to understand what the status of rapper consists of at this particular historical moment. This requires that we attend to the economic, social, and political stakes at play in this field.

In this chapter I aim to examine the social position of the rapper in contemporary London, beginning with a discussion of the representation of everyday life in London through rap music. I connect the particularity of experience represented in lyrics to the city's history of black labour migration, racist social and economic marginalisation, and the ongoing inner-city poverty in which working-class blacks dwell. I then discuss the significance of black youths' linguistic resistance to their marginalisation and the participation of white working-class youths in London's black cultural scenes. Through an examination of 'hustling' by working-class artists, both black and white, I investigate the postcolonial character of the city and consider the MC's role in the organisation of social consciousness in the capital. Following this, I analyse the strategies employed by rap artists in the representation of urban poverty and the difficulties that they face in their engagement with social malaise and political disconnection in their local communities. In connection with these difficulties I undertake an examination of competing representations of life in London by UK hip-hop and grime artists. These representations are used in the construction of social identity in the capital and are bound up in social agents' struggles to accommodate themselves to the conditions they inhabit. Consequently, my examination of these representations engages with the role that they play in urban youths' challenges to their marginalisation and rappers' attempts to make a living for themselves. I then move on to consider the strategies employed by artists in the pursuit of economic autonomy and the ethical values invoked in the construction of the identities of the MC and DJ. These identities are constituted through a negotiation with artists' interpretative communities. I analyse how struggles over the terms through which rap music is valued form part of rap artists' negotiation of their relationships with their work and with their audiences. The chapter concludes with a discussion of the significance of the distinct social and aesthetic positions adopted by artists in the black public sphere. By attending to a range of strategies employed by artists, in interviews, rap lyrics, and music videos, I attempt to engage with the social, political, and cultural significance of contemporary London's rappers and of the city's rap music scenes.

PARTICULARITY AND SELF-REPRESENTATION

In tracks such as 'Junior Spesh' and 'Lidl,' Red Hot and Afrikan Boy represent their everyday experiences and circumstances. Rather than adopting a generic blackness from globalised US hip-hop culture, these artists use their work to express themselves and their local particularity. Klayze recalls how his crew made 'Junior Spesh':

> It kind of started off as a joke. The studio was at Jaxor's house and just across the road from Jaxor's house was this chicken and chip shop that everyone just used to go to before we go there, or after we go there, or

whilst we're there, and get on with it—just go to the chicken and chip shop. Get a Junior Spesh, its like £1.50, and its just, its like a quick meal and everyone would like do that while they were hungry. And people would make up silly rhymes about it but nothing serious. Then X-Ray got the beat, we found a beat for it, then certain people came up with little verses, rhymes and stuff, and we just put it together and that's what happened.

Using jokes and observations about their everyday lives and their local area is part of the process through which emerging artists position themselves in this field and distinguish themselves from others. In a similar manner, Afrikan Boy takes particular issues from the world around him and presents these to his public. Rejecting a generic blackness, he speaks the truth of his experience. In 'Lidl' he expresses his consciousness of his particular position in society and his attempts to accommodate himself to it. While in these songs Red Hot and Afrikan Boy deal with their conditions of urban dwelling through humour, Ty identifies how inner-city poverty affected social life in South London:

South London is pocketed. So its like, it depends on who you are with, who you know, and who you associate with, as in regards to the danger aspects. But you can see Piranhas walking the pavement, but you pretty much can avoid them. That's South London for me. You can avoid Piranhas if you so wish. There's a—also there's a sense of history in South. I come from Brixton so, there's just a sense—I was there when the Brixton riots was happening—when I say I was there, I was being looked after, being baby sat in someone's house—I remember watching it on TV. And South London—Brixton's tough, if you grew up in Brixton in the last 20 years it's tough, because it's not—it's full on. It's—you're gonna get into scrapes eventually.

Ty's perspective of his social world foregrounds the harshness of contemporary life on Brixton's streets and historically connects this to the rebellions of the 1980s. Having grown up in the Myatts Field Estate, he observes a 'toughness' in the 'spirit' of his local area. In order to characterise life in his city he compares having to tell 'some yardie guy' to 'back off,' with the hustle of using the London Underground: 'It's like the tube, sometimes you're gonna get pushed and pulled around. . . . Brixton's like that all the time. But not—But its like that spiritually.'

I want to consider this social dissonance alongside the effects of the racial division of labour and wagelessness on young black men during the 1970s that Hall et al. discuss in *Policing the Crisis*. Arguing that this marginalised group cannot be considered part of the lumpenproletariat in the classic Marxist sense, Hall et al. (1978: 375) highlight the necessity of looking at the historical development of this class fraction in the Caribbean, and later in the UK, as part of a reserve army of labour. In this text, Darcus Howe describes how in the Caribbean this section of the class subsists by ' "eking out" a survival in a wageless world, *not*, usually, by resorting to crime' (emphasis in text):

> What normally happens in those days would be somehow your whole personality develops skills by which you get portions of the wage. Either by using your physical strength as a gang leader, or your cunning—so that section of the working class is disciplined by that general term and form called 'hustling'.
>
> (Hall et al. 1978: 373)

Without suggesting any simple political parallels, *Policing the Crisis* examines the manner in which this section of the population was incorporated into the metropolitan economy as a vulnerable class fraction, in order to explain the response of young black men to the social and economic pressures that acted upon them. What is of importance to the present study is how the continued vulnerability of this section of the working class influences the production of contemporary rap. Howe states that 'the unemployed I talk about in the Caribbean, that has not got a wage, an official wage of any kind, no wealth, is a vibrant powerful section of society. It has always been that. Culturally, steel band, Calypso, reggae come from that section of the population.' Through rap, a marginalised group of people pronounce upon their experience and conditions with the cultural resources at their disposal. It is clear from Ty's remarks above that the working-class environment in which he grew up was 'tough.' His sense of history draws on the rebellious response in Brixton to the metropolitan police's institutional racism in order to convey the spirit of toughness in the area. Red Hot's jokes about purchasing cheap food and Afrikan Boy's comic portrayal of shop-lifting in response to his student poverty—'EMA didn't pay me'—depict the experience of a younger generation in the city and how they deal with the pressures that come to bear upon them. These rappers draw attention to contemporary issues of social marginalisation and economic deprivation through resources that have been cultivated within the black public sphere.

Elijah Anderson's seminal study of Philadelphia and his concept of a 'code of the street' may be usefully compared to contemporary London and the conditions that Ty describes. Anderson places this 'code of the streets' within the socioeconomic conditions of Philadelphia's inner-city poor:

> The inclination to violence springs from the circumstances of life among the ghetto poor—the lack of jobs that pay a living wage, limited basic public services . . ., the stigma of race, the fallout of rampant drug use and drug trafficking, and the resulting alienation and absence of hope for the future. Simply living in such an environment places young people at

special risk of falling victim to aggressive behaviour. . . . Above all, this environment means that even youngsters whose home lives reflect mainstream values—and most of the homes in the community do—must be able to handle themselves in a street-oriented environment.

(Anderson 2000: 32)

Ty's recollection of his local area relates social tensions to limited opportunities and the risks of urban dwelling that resemble the conditions that Anderson describes:

> It was tense, you know, everyone was doing what they were doing, you kind of learned not to look at people in the face for too long, but you learned to look at people in their eye long enough to make them realise that you're not scared of them. . . . Coming out of my house you put a mask on, and you go about your business. . . . There were people that were loafing, there were people that were studying, there were people that were working, there were people that were becoming parents, and then there was crack. . . . I've had multiple scenario's where crack—where I'm actually seeing people that I know, that I've grown up with or people that I used to look up to, people that I used to buy records from when I first started sampling, my first love interest, er, some kids I used to look after, I saw on the street the other day and I was like 'she's a crack-head and a prostitute, wow! How did that happen?' Do you know what I mean? That's my area.

Although Anderson identifies the need to provide a structural context, his own analysis tends to emphasise the position of the 'code' within the immediate cultural context rather than its relations to structural changes in society. Statements such as '[t]he code of the streets and the world it reflects have taken shape in the context of the existing structures and traditions in the black community in the United States' (Anderson: 179) place the discursive layer of the code within the context of a black tradition. The layers of signification at times eclipse the material position of the people Anderson observes. Similarly, Ty's comments deal with the immediacy of his lived experience and the accumulation of his direct observations over time. However, it is necessary to go further than Anderson's minimal effort to bear in mind the economic shifts 'from manufacturing to a service and high-tech economy in which the well-being of workers, particularly those with low skills and little education, is subordinated to the bottom line' (Anderson 2000: 110). The adoption of Anderson's study by the US Department of Justice signals its influence on policymakers and criminal courts.[2] Consequently, it is necessary to challenge his emphasis on the cultural, and to firmly locate the position of poor, working-class blacks within the context of structural subordination. Their cultural production will then be more properly understood as a response to their socioeconomic conditions.

Hall noted that Britain's black settler population provided 'the sector of labour subject to the *highest* rate of exploitation' (Hall et al. 1978: 344). As employment deepened during the economic crisis of the 1970s, 'those heading for the bottom end of the labouring pile become the unemployed reserve army of labour' (Hall et al. 1978: 356). The vulnerability of blacks within the global labour market led to the conditions of poverty and worklessness witnessed by Ty and experienced in his community. In addition to considering how shifts in the global economy come to bear upon urban youths, Ty's comments should also be placed within the context of structural racism. Hall observed that in 'relation to black youth, the education system has served effectively to depress the opportunities for employment and education advancement, and has therefore resulted in "reproducing" the young black worker as labour at the lower end of employment, production and skill' (Hall et al. 1978: 340). The shortage of school places in Lambeth during the period Ty grew up, along with the selling off of local schools by the council in order to allow property developers to build luxury apartments in the borough, formed part of the background to the social tensions he witnessed. The underinvestment in local education facilities, along with the structural unemployment of blacks, were significant aspects of the socioeconomic and political context that would have come to bear upon him and others in his area. Following the financial crisis in 2008, Lambeth's Labour-run council planned to dispose of educational buildings even as it recognised the lack of sufficient primary school places for children in the borough.[3] The Labour MP, Kate Hoey, condemned the plan as 'short-sighted' and argued that 'Lambeth should not revisit its mistakes of the past by selling off educational buildings only to discover later the need for more school places.'[4]

In contrast to the black ghettos that Anderson focussed on in Philadelphia, the estates that Ty describes and the areas in which Red Hot and Afrikan Boy live are ethnically diverse. The participation of artists such as Scratchy and Devlin in the grime scene is brought about by the close proximity of working- and underclass blacks and whites to one another. F recalls his interest in black culture while growing up in the 1980s.[5] He describes how he got involved in rapping and the way that the culture relieved the pressures of chronic poverty:

> F: The street culture is mixed, always. . . . The crew we rolled with was always mixed. . . . Highbury is a very mixed, kind of diverse area of cultures—as is London. . . . From my own personal point of view I had a hangup about class. . . . Being from very low-class family, not even working class, *lower* class. I used to rob people who I knew were of a different class to me. I didn't, I didn't socialise with people from a different class. . . . I was one of those people who was always a victim, but at the same time always—what do you call it—an aggressor. Because of what I was and what I did, in secondary school, I was like 'I wanna be down.'

So I had to go through so much shit. It was militant back then. . . . The black kids were militant. . . . I was a white guy, I was trying to do my rapping and people didn't like me, a lot of the black guys didn't like me. . . . So they'd beat me up. They'd rob me, they'd make me do shit . . . prove myself. . . . I know we all went through it, I'm sure Skinny went through it 'cause we all come from those kind of areas . . . (F's emphasis).

RB: So, why did you want to hang around with them?

F: The funk man, there was something musically. . . . It was probably the culture of music, and the dancing, and the weed, and just the whole—there was something that drew me to it.

Growing up in chronic urban poverty F observed and participated in robbery and violence with other white and black youths. He also recalls alienated white youths stealing buses and diggers to display them, driving around the estate. His characterisation of the people that made up his local area conveys a need for recognition expressed in these acts of criminality. F's description suggests that despite the aggressive manner of those he socialised with, certain elements in the black culture offered some relief from the boredom, poverty, and alienation from society he and others experienced: 'I was just attracted to it. I don't know why. Rather that then me be like one of the, attracted to the white kind of—the white kids in my school were fucking nuts.'

F and his friends used rap to develop supportive relations with other youths and the skills to express themselves. Their participation in this culture also provided them with the resources to begin to deal with their structural economic position. F describes how he and his crew funded the production and distribution of their album:

We didn't really fund it to be honest. We just adopted all of our—street knowledge—knowing how to sell and make a profit. Knowing how to buy something, chop it into little bits, sell it for more. All that kind of knowledge that enables you to have half of a business mind. . . . We met up with Joe Christie, Braintax, I met him in the old Mr. Bongos, in West End. And I had a chat with him, got on very well, and I propositioned him with an idea, that I wanna put out a series of CDs. . . . We're gonna record them at home, there'll be no recording costs. We'll bring it to you on a CD. . . . I said to him how much is it gonna cost for 5,000 CDs. He said its gonna cost this much. I said well you front the money, we'll make the money back, we'll give you that much, and we'll give you 50 pence, £1, per CD off the sales. So we'd sell that 5,000, he'd make himself £5,000 for manufacturing CDs and lending us the money. So it worked for all of us.

London's economic condition has considerably developed in the decades since F first began to rap. Along with the city's widening economic inequality there remain substantial pockets of poverty, worklessness, and alienation, which contribute to the drug use and social malaise that Ty describes in contemporary Brixton. Aspects of these conditions are depicted in songs by Red Hot and Afrikan Boy and in Devlin's social commentary in 'Community Outcast.' Devlin's offering depicts a young father who is demonised for claiming unemployment benefit—'the government says that his family are spongers'—within an economic context in which 'he got taken off site because its cheaper to pay Europeans to labour in numbers.' The depiction of poverty, homelessness, and social isolation, alongside images of white families and black children, foregrounds the plight of marginalised, working-class communities. The reference to Europeans in this representation of solidarity between England's working-class blacks and whites identifies the new patterns of labour migration and conveys a sense of the changed value of whiteness in the United Kingdom's capital city.

UK HIP-HOP AND GRIME: LINGUISTIC RESISTANCE THEN AND NOW

It is important to recall Hall's analysis in *Policing the Crisis* in the consideration of the political significance of investing one's self in becoming an MC or DJ in contemporary London. The failure of schools during the 1970s to reflect pupils' cultural backgrounds in their teaching, even where the children attending were predominantly black, has had a substantial bearing upon London's character. Hall observed that black schoolchildren's '*resistance through language* marks out the school as, quite literally, a cultural battleground' (Hall et al. 1978: 341, emphasis in text). When rapping takes place in schools today, teachers' responses can differ considerably. In his description of his teachers' attempts to restructure the organisation of MCing in the playground, Klayze contrasts a certainty of feeling and being, in the circle, with the unreliable (and unknowing, but nevertheless controlling) view of teachers outside the circle:

> KLAYZE: It was all really friendly, like competitive kind of thing. It was a main attraction kind of thing. . . . There would be a big group of them in the playground, just like in a huddle, and I'd be the Year 7 just trying to get in and push through the crowd and see what's going on. And it was always a really lively kind of thing. But it wasn't really—the teachers weren't fond of it cause it seemed like—I don't know what it was that they didn't like about it. I didn't know if it was the fact that it just looked like trouble—and then obviously when certain MCs get the hype, and everyone's kind of shouting and making noise, its kind of—I don't know what it was.
>
> RB: Did they take any active steps to stop it?

KLAYZE: They kind of said 'oh, you can't do that' or 'you can't stand around in groups,' but people still found ways to do it.

Teachers' actions had the effect of distancing the culture of the pupils from that of the school. They also had an impact on the feeling that was produced through their activity. Rather than being immersed in what Klayze describes as 'the passion of it,' participants became concerned with whether teachers would come and break them up. In contrast, Afrikan Boy describes the incorporation of grime into his school's teaching:

> For me the most memorable moment was when I did Music Tech and I made this beat, it was grime with oriental-influenced music, and then I spat lyrics over it. And up to this day the music teacher still plays it as an example . . . it's nice to know that I left a mark on my old school.

These teachers' contrary responses to rapping may suggest ways in which social and educational policy could be developed. Hall identifies an inherent cultural bias in the formal education system, in which 'the reproduction of educational disadvantage for blacks is accomplished, in part, through a variety of racially specific mechanisms. The "cultural capital" of this sector is constantly expropriated, often unwittingly, through its practical devaluation' (Hall et al. 1978: 340). Clearly, educational institutions have not yet found effective strategies through which these common cultural practices may be systematically converted into educational capital. However, for the present study it is more important to note that regardless of the response of the institution, the activity of rapping endured within it and outside it. The substantial difference to the participants is that in one school their passion was allowed to leave its mark, in order to further motivate others in their educational and cultural development.

The phenomenon of young, white, working-class men such as F, and later Scratchy and Devlin, participating in the black cultural tradition is testimony to the longevity of this strategy of linguistic resistance. It is just as significant that in the historical moment in which Hall wrote, he also observed that there 'are specific mechanisms which serve to reproduce what almost appears to be a "racial division of labour" within, and as a structural feature of, the general division of labour' (Hall et al. 1978: 345). Alongside the 'numbers in the "colony" living off hustling [which had] increased steadily with the rising curve of black unemployment' that Hall et al. (353) observed in their analysis, working-class white youths found resources within black culture that enabled them to deal with their own position (Hewitt 1986: 137). In F's case this culture offered relief from the pressures of chronic poverty and social marginalisation. Hall goes on to state: 'Another class of person drawn into hustling are those who simply cannot or will not subject themselves to steady, routine kinds of labouring for "the Man". They prefer to risk their fortunes working the street than take in the white Man's "shit-work", or sit it out in his dole queues' (353). F's comments above reveal how the street culture of the 1980s provided the occasion for alienated young men of various ethnic backgrounds to come into contact with one another, and in his experience class antagonisms took precedence over any difference in 'race.' Furthermore, rap provided means through which he and his white, black, and Asian friends took their hustling into the sphere of art.

In contemporary London's grime scene, it is possible to trace an ethic of self-sufficiency and a resistance to accepting a position of alienated subordination. However, the aesthetic and economic dynamism of grime contrasts with Britain's hip-hop scene, which F now dismisses as 'niche,' 'contrived,' 'small minded,' and 'regulated.' His characterisation of UK hip-hop may be usefully compared to Fanon's description of national culture under colonisation: 'There is merely a clinging to a nucleus which is increasingly shrivelled, increasingly inert, and increasingly hollow' (2004: 172). This husk of a culture signals the lack of vitality in the generic forms of blackness represented through commercialised US hip-hop culture. In contrast to the grime scene, UK hip-hop's strong identification with American culture has, consequently, contributed to its own decline. F's concern that UK hip-hop is no longer 'rebellious' is expressed in his observation that 'the hip-hop music that we listen to and that we make and the crowds and the fans that go to the concerts all regulate themselves within what is considered the rules.' This ossification within generic forms of blackness contrasts with grime's fluidity and range of exploration.

HUSTLING: SOCIAL ENTERPRISE AND BLACK POLITICAL CULTURE

Ty and F's comments regarding growing up in Brixton and Highbury depict social marginalisation, poverty, and a toughness that characterised the culture of their local communities. In particular, F recalls being subject to beatings by older boys, black and white, in order to be accepted by them: 'It was a test, it was a trial for me, and I got through it.' There are similarities between the toughness that they experienced and the 'code of the streets' that Andersen discusses. However, in order to deal with the potential political significance of the activities of these cultural entrepreneurs, and those who followed them, it is necessary to draw attention to some of the weaknesses in Anderson's study. By focussing almost exclusively on cultural issues and their relation to violence, Anderson downplays how this street culture manifests the adaptation of this marginalised social group to the economic conditions that black urban youths are forced to inhabit. By opposing this code to the 'decent' people who maintain black traditions, he obscures how the actions of young men and women constitute adaptations of this very tradition to their present conditions. Furthermore, he overlooks the collective failure of the 'decent' people to come to terms with the conditions that the whole community faces.

Anderson frequently elides acts that impact negatively on other members of the black community when they are committed by those who represent themselves (or that he wants to represent) as decent. The use of the term 'decent' constructs a privileged position through its moral valuation. That moral dimension problematises his attempts to draw attention to wider socioeconomic structures in order to provide an explanatory context. His use of the term also compromises his analysis of the social barriers constructed by 'decent' blacks in order to protect their economic interests. Anderson fails to make explicit the existence of a generational division of labour that relegated young black men to life on the streets of Philadelphia and without access to the jobs through which they might gain the social respect given to 'decent' members of the community. Anderson's maintenance of the 'street/ decent' binary and his overlooking of the counterproductive acts of 'decent' people are connected to his erasure of class differences and his more blatant avoidance of the impact of racism on the communities on which he focusses. The institutionally racist arrangements that consign blacks to the worst jobs (when any are available) placed some older black men in a position in which they were able to police those who had access to even the most menial work. Finally, Anderson seems to identify the middle classes only through a value system that is adopted by 'decent' people, rather than with a socioeconomic position that is denied blacks in the impoverished community that he studies. He does not even account for this in his conclusion (in which he does give some consideration to the economic context), but instead calls for more jobs for blacks without addressing how they are denied them in the first instance.

Hall's analysis of the social and economic conditions in which blacks dwell contrasts with Anderson's emphasis on a cultural code. Hall observed that as a result of the way particular structures work together, race becomes the 'principle modality in which black members of that class "live", experience, make sense of and thus *come to a consciousness* of their structured subordination' (Hall et al. 1978: 347, emphasis in text). This allows us to see how F's adaptation of street knowledge to more legitimate pursuits represents not solely cultural conflict but also political struggle: 'It is through the modality of race that blacks comprehend, handle and then begin to resist the exploitation which is an objective feature of their class situation.' F and Devlin's appropriation of black culture complicates the scheme that I am trying to outline here, but I want to make that complication apparent from the outset. F did not simply use rap to express the problems that he faced. He developed his awareness of his position in a multicultural environment, and rap was one of the means through which his consciousness of subordination was developed. Hall identified 'hustling' as a response to the structural forces that relegated blacks to a reserve army of labour and assigned them to the lowest-paid and most insecure work. What is important to the present study is Hall's analysis of the significance of 'the growing "refusal to work."' This refusal is of 'one of the principal defining structures of the system—its productive relations, which have systematically assigned the black worker to the ranks of the deskilled labourer' (Hall et al. 1978: 391). I will consider below how UK hip-hop and grime artists put this refusal into practice in contemporary London. However, prior to engaging with this economic strategy it is worthwhile considering the possibilities and limitations of attempts to mobilise rap in order to effect social change at the cultural level.

Daz, like other DJs and producers, such as Dexplicit, also engaged with schools and other statutory organisations. In one case he worked 'with Waltham Forest council . . . going around to various youth clubs, I was giving them like, kids that come to the youth clubs, advice on how to get into the music game.' MCs and DJs' social and cultural capital is used by local authorities to engage with the children that they have a duty of care for. Seeker discusses how, through his creative writing classes for Haringey council, he attempted to reshape the consciousness of these children:

> We used to do classes, creative writing classes and MC classes, and one of the things we had was a strictly positive lyric [rule]. And the young people we had, sometimes we had 20 young people around one mic, and they would struggle. Because the lyrics that they had written was all about baseball bats and protecting my area and my postcode, don't come to my ends and—so the lyrics weren't, weren't appropriate. And we had an event where we encourage these young people to write positive lyrics and we'd then explain to them 'well since you've got those positive lyrics now you can actually perform on stage. Because the people you're gonna be performing for—there's gonna be children there, there's gonna be adults there.' And if you can look at an artist and say 'right, are these lyrics that you're gonna be able to rap in front of your parents, would you rap these in front of your mum?' And they'd say 'no.' 'So then why would you write something like that?' So they would say that's actually the fashion trend. I would say, 'I write how I feel.' I don't want to say 'write what's real,' because for some of the young people those are the lives that they live . . . in a violent sense.

Although Seeker's methods imposed certain constraints on those he worked with, in exchange for offering them a platform, he recognised the problems of using rap as a form of expression where this produced lyrics that were 'not appropriate' to be presented to their wider community. Working over the short term at the level of cultural output could do nothing to change the underlying conditions that produced such lyrics. Nevertheless, within the aims of this project these urban youths eventually performed 'positive' lyrics in front of their local community. Through this they also developed their awareness of their artistic potential and creative range.

Seeker's motivation of children and young adults to write 'positive' lyrics is developed through his own creative output. He challenges perceptions of what a black man can say, and how urban youths may express themselves. He describes his rap song 'Mama' as an apology and thank you to his mother 'for the pain and—you know—but also for still believing in me regardless of what's happened.' After performing this song at a school he noticed a 14-year-old girl crying, who, he learned, had been arrested a few days earlier following a fight. The girl told him that she was going to go home and apologise to her mother. But when he saw her again, outside, he noticed a 'front' that the girl was still trying to maintain.

> Her eyes were still glazing and she was like 'I don't want people to see me like this.' It just makes you realise how much front needs to be put by the young people. So that self-image that they have of themselves, or want to show, they feel they can't really show that, so up comes a barrier. So going into schools and trying to break down that barrier—it's hard. But its about, I think, building up relationships, and when you're getting the young people to express themselves, sometimes the things they come out with, it lets you know how much they have bottled inside.

I suggest that the construction of this 'front' is an important part of the development of an adult identity, as well as a response to the social pressures Seeker's 'young people' face. His work attempts to reconstruct the way in which they relate to themselves through their cultural production. He attempts to 'break down' the 'barriers' that these children construct in response to the conditions in which they live. This is coupled with the idealism of his aim of encouraging these urban youths to write 'positive' lyrics, even where he recognises the links between 'negative' lyrics and lived experience. In spite of his admirable aims, working at this level does not engage with the socioeconomic conditions in which these boys and girls find themselves, or 'what's real' to them. Indeed, while he may direct them away from the absurd reification of postcode identities, his work also has a role in distracting marginalised youths from the socioeconomic forces that act upon them and the conditions in which they dwell. Nevertheless, the response of these children to his efforts demonstrates that, by working at the level of cultural production, he is able to engage them on their terms and begin to broaden their categories of perception and appreciation.

In spite of Seeker's success in producing positive performances by children in front of their parents and local community, he still faced opposition in his attempt to develop his community politics:

> Even for years we were fighting to get a studio. But strangely enough it was the local residents who didn't want it. Simply because they felt that you were gonna have your typical group of young people, in hoods, gathered around, up to no good. And we were trying to say 'well,

no. What we want to do is give young people a chance to express themselves, to be creative, in the elements that they love.'

This resulted in some youths' becoming uninterested in working with him (youths he believed could have been engaged earlier). Instead, they were now 'hanging out on the streets' while 'pursuing careers of becoming artists, some of them, but not the most positive of artists.' Seeker's objectives, like Anderson's, are focussed at the cultural level, rather than the underlying conditions. However, in contrast to Anderson, Seeker identifies the effect of the community's actions in marginalising young people's cultural production to the streets. An important gain for him in what he referred to as this 'struggle' was obtaining funding for recording equipment for the community centre that he runs. Although those resources fell far short of a studio, Seeker was able to teach young people how to use the equipment. They also gained the opportunity to record some of their creative output without paying upwards of £15 per hour at a commercial studio.

It is important to acknowledge Seeker's contribution in supporting young people to develop their creative output and teaching them how to use advanced technologies. Through this social and cultural engagement they acquired valuable skills that may be employed in London's high-tech economy. This work is consistent with his role as a 'conscious rapper.' His efforts to organise and represent his community are connected to his insistence that 'I don't want to write music just for it to sell.' They are directed to social and cultural, rather than economic, aspirations. Nevertheless, a focus on 'positive' lyrics cannot tackle the underlying conditions that give rise to 'inappropriate' lyrics. I maintain that Seeker's aversion to grime, coupled with his focus on being 'positive,' cannot engage with the problematics posed by grime and confronted in the social world from which it springs. His admirable efforts to broaden the categories of perception and the range of content that young people employ do not address the economic challenges that Daz and JJ's modes of cultural production set out to deal with. Tackling the underlying causes of 'negative' lyrics and changing the way marginalised people express themselves require long-term engagement with the 'negative' social and economic forces that come to bear upon these aspiring artists.

REPPING FOR THE BLOCK

For JJ a 'grimey lifestyle' is 'typical East London, even London life depending where abouts in London you're from. Fast paced kind of lifestyle, cheap kind of lifestyle . . . it's a hustle, it's not easy. A majority of people who do this music have to put in a lot before they get anything out.' He goes on to say that 'it's a 140bpm kind of lifestyle which is the tempo of the music.' The intensity of experience represented through grime music is bound up with the forces that structure the conditions of urban dwelling, to which

JJ refers. In the critical engagement with rap music videos that I undertake below, I aim to connect these cultural products with the social and economic conditions of their production. In doing so I will pursue an interpretative agenda that is sensitive to the complexities and ambivalences of these cultural works. The opposition from residents that Seeker confronted when attempting to obtain equipment to provide a studio for local children reveals how difficult expressing the significance of the issues that they face can be in his position. Nevertheless, I argue that engagement with young people's cultural production needs to go deeper than producing 'positive' lyrics. It needs to engage with 'what's real' to them, the predispositions that make up their *habitus*, and how they may develop their cultural production in a manner that works through the problematic conditions that they face.

As I listened to the 'Grimey Breakfast' show on the pirate radio station Rinse FM one morning, Scratcha asked his audience 'do you think the Queen wipes her own bum?' His decision to broadcast this vulgar question followed the release on YouTube of 'Jerusalem' by MC Nobody (known more widely as Sway). The video shows the MC, whose face is concealed by a black balaclava, kidnapping the monarch from a school assembly in which a black boy sings William Blake's hymn, 'Jerusalem.' Scenes of the Queen being taken through supermarkets, council estates, pubs, streets, and various domestic settings, including the toilet, are accompanied by MC Nobody's social commentary on the state of the nation. He tells his audience: 'I can take you where the Queen ain't never been, and Gordon B ain't never seen.' The Queen's position is lowered by placing her in everyday situations, and these incongruous images give force to the rapper's critique. The video places into question the relation between the nation's elite and people's everyday lives. Through the grotesque aesthetic that lowers the Queen, placing her on a toilet instead of a throne, Nobody draws attention to the condition of England. His rap attempts to rehabilitate ideas of political accountability and leadership, social and economic responsibility, and communal life.

Sway's use of this vernacular art form in his critique of the state of the nation should be distinguished from other vernacular developments. One of the significant trends within the grime scene is an emphasis placed on a far more restricted political identity: the postcode. The opening of the Southside Allstars' track 'Southside Riddim' features a succession of MCs stating their names and the area that they are representing, along with the corresponding postcode. Given the decline in letter writing in British culture and the rise in the use of electronic communication, the take up of this protocol of identification is somewhat difficult to understand. It is perhaps too easy to identify American hip-hop songs such as Ludacris's 'Area Codes' as contributing to this development. That would overlook grime's distinctive characteristics. It would also obscure the possibility that the use of 'road' as an alternative vernacular expression to 'street' did more than distinguish the local grime scene from globalised hip-hop. The presence of postcodes on road signs may have been one way in which groups of marginalised youths sought to define themselves against others. It also highlights grime's relation to a social world in which value is placed on the connection between locality and identity. This trend is reinforced in a city that discourages children from use of the underground tube network and in which young people find themselves ghettoised in small areas of poverty. The Southside Allstars' track responds to the identification of the grime scene with East London. The presence of Asher D, formerly of the So Solid Crew, in the video allows those dwelling in South London (and represented through the video) some claim to having 'started the flow,' or cultural tributary, to the grime aesthetic employed in the soundtrack.

The connection of grime to local schools and youth centres did not ensure the development towards postcode particularism. However, the limited opportunities available to young people to participate in the life of the city as a whole may have increased its likelihood. Although free bus passes make travel in the city more accessible, the high prices demanded by many attractions limit the value of this entitlement. Ty's comments about his local area are relevant to this issue, as is Hall's analysis of the 'colony' area in Britain. I suggest that the economic and social barriers that face marginalised youths have contributed to the limited movement of these young people in the city and, consequently, the narrowing of the social and geographical space with which they identify. Grime expresses the fast-paced, hustling lifestyle of those who dwell within London's colony areas. However, this mode of urban dwelling is itself a response to the narrow economic opportunities faced by young working-class people and the contracted forms of sociality that racism produces. The historical causes of this shrinking of political identity are complex, and the issue goes beyond the scope of this study. However, its development signals the limited value of any argument about the state of the nation in relation to contemporary rap music cultures. The participation of blacks and whites in this video emphasises that these contracted identities prioritise locality over nation or race.

One of Seeker's criticisms of grime associates the genre with violent crime and the 'effect of music on young people.' He did not identify grime in its totality with violence, but pointed out a number of grime artists whose music dealt with violence. Directing children to 'positive' lyrics, or prohibiting them from writing 'negative' lyrics in the space that he provides, is the strategy that he employs to deal with 'violence' in lyrical content, rather than in the social world they inhabit. This does not directly equate to censorship. However, it can be compared with the actions of the metropolitan police to discourage particular types of music in London, which does amount to informal state censorship. In an interview with New Musical Express (NME), and then posted on DJ Semtex's blog, Giggs discussed the effect of having been convicted for possession of a firearm on his attempt to use a career in music to begin anew:

'. . . when labels were looking to sign me,' Giggs tells us, 'and before XL signed me, everyone wanted to have a go. Trident rang up every single one of them telling them about my past, and how they shouldn't have anything to do with me. They shut down my shows. Every single thing I do that's supposed to be positive they fuck up for me. It's as if they don't want me to make legal money. It's as if they want me to end up back on streets or something! Why wouldn't you want someone to do something positive? I've learnt my lesson and done my time in Jail.' Giggs frustrations were capped when the intervention of Trident last year meant a Lil Wayne support slot had to be aborted.[6]

This intervention by the police raises important issues about how people are reintegrated into society after they are punished. It also indicates the suppression of the freedom that marginalised people have to represent their experiences.

These issues need to be looked at critically, along with how the metropolitan police's regime of risk assessments limits who may perform at events in the capital. The development of that extralegal measure after grime's emergence and its refinement during the financial crisis have significantly impacted upon black artists. A disproportionate number of events were cancelled in the boroughs of Newham and Lambeth, in East and South London, following assessment by the police. Giggs's rap lyrics depict a mode of life in Peckham, in which possession of a weapon is not uncommon. However, the suppression of music that deals with these issues does not address the underlying causes of social violence, possession of weapons, or other issues faced by those who dwell in areas of deprivation. Instead, it suppresses engagement with the social and economic issues that confront marginalised groups.

Following widespread outcry about the murder of teenagers in London, a number of artists, including Sway and Sincere, released songs that dealt with the issue of knife violence in the city. Importantly, the emphasis of these songs was on violence in life rather than on representations of violence in music. Those critiques of social violence also challenged racism, unjust policing, and government indifference to the plight of the people. Giggs, Sincere, and Sway's representations form part of an ongoing process in which this sector of the working class recognises and depicts its position within the wider social whole. It is clear from Giggs's interview that his attempt at developing a music career was directed towards making money legitimately. Given the limited economic opportunities for marginalised blacks during periods of high unemployment, the metropolitan police's suppression of black popular culture raises urgent questions about how marginalised groups are enabled to support themselves economically and how free they are to represent or contest their marginality.

The work of people such as Daz and Seeker must be supported, but not uncritically. Their efforts help urban youths develop the cultural resources they use to deal with the conditions in which they live. However, despite Seeker's acknowledgement of the socioeconomic problems underlying some of the content of young artists' rap lyrics, his work is principally focussed on the cultural level. Given the opposition that he faced in his attempt to build a studio, obtaining the additional resources needed to tackle the economic and social issues to which his cultural work is related requires informed critical analysis of the role of rap music in urban life. The difficulty of winning local support for community projects is exacerbated by a substantial gap between the common cultural level that Seeker is engaged in and the world of the policymakers who create the administrative and funding structures through which he must work.

It is worth briefly considering the relation of these policymakers to marginalised youths. Seeker described an event in which he and other artists performed for the Office of Deputy Prime Minister (ODPM), after receiving an award for work funded through the Single Regeneration Budget scheme:

> Here you had a group of black children in front of suits and it was like spot the black, seriously. They loved it, you know. So we were coming with a hip-hop element. Now a lot of these people, you could tell were used to seeing just the negative—fingers being pointed towards black children. By the way they approached us afterwards, it was with this shocking, you know, expression and surprise—that we were positive in our elements, so well mannered.

He was pleased with the response of the 'suits,' but noticed their lack of ease when talking with him and his associates:

> It was just beautiful to have them come up to us, congratulate us. And actually observing them almost building up a sort of—a sort of means of how to approach us. They didn't know how to actually, you know, if they could just come over and talk to us. . . . I've even been in a situation where it's like 'it's very rare to see, you know, coloured people' and it was just like 'pardon?' and I started laughing and she was, she felt a bit uncomfortable, because she could see she used a term that wasn't common. And I just comforted her and said 'you know don't worry, its cool.' So it definitely can educate people if they're willing to listen.

The social and cultural distance that Seeker observed between himself and those present at the performance for John Prescott's ODPM indicates the substantial disconnect between policymakers and the urban youths that Seeker works with. This highlights that effective engagement is unlikely to take place through the policies of this disconnected political class. Far closer attention needs to be directed to the efforts of committed cultural practitioners and community activists in dealing with the social and economic conditions expressed through Britain's vernacular cultures. This must then be followed by effective engagement from policymakers with young people's needs.

'EVOLVE OR BE EXTINCT'

In contrast to Devlin's critique of government neglect and Afrikan Boy's description of shop-lifting in response to his experience of poverty, the video for Wiley's 2004 single 'Wot Do U Call It?' depicts an alternative mode of economic subsistence that avoids the stigma associated with claiming government benefits. In order to deal with their marginal social and economic position, Wiley and the motley Roll Deep crew turn to making music. The video shows him bringing a box into a record shop before shifting to a scene in which he raps into a microphone in a studio. This is followed by a series of shots in a record press. Significantly, after Wiley is depicted shaking hands with the manager, who gives him a box of records that have, presumably, been paid for, the video shows one of the members of the crew stealing another box as they walk out of the press. The scene foregrounds the crew's opportunistic activities and their position in the margin of the legitimate economy. Wiley's rap celebrates his success in producing a distinctive sound, which distinguishes his work from other musical genres. Closing with scenes of him celebrating in a club after a performance, the video represents Wiley as a successful cultural entrepreneur. The rap song and its accompanying video foreground the specificity of the MC's social world and his cultural production. Far from representing rap in an idealist or Romantic sense, it is portrayed in the context of a number of businesses and as an economic activity in itself. The hustling that is represented by the theft of the records draws the legitimate economic production of music closer to the illegitimate economic activity of 'street culture.' That culture is also invoked through scenes of motorbikes racing down a public road. The video thematises the distinctions produced through the position that Wiley takes in his cultural production: his relation to other music scenes, a social world in which being quick-witted and opportunistic is valued, and the economic value of his rapping.

This representation of the grime scene's development may be compared with Wiley's 'Cash In My Pocket,' released in 2008. The video opens with a scene of two men in business suits driving through the Bishopsgate area of London. Set mainly in an office, the song describes how Wiley has found that 'music is paying me well' and his determination to secure his income: '[W]hen I get one I'm gonna put away half.' The wealth that he boasts he is able to maintain into the 'next year, next year, next year, next year and the year after' contrasts with the fortunes of the financial sector. The video closes with an image of a falling stock market ticker and a red chart. The release of this track during the global financial crisis is significant. It may be usefully connected to Fanon's identification that the emergence of tensions in colonial systems is registered within colonised cultures. 'Once a pale imitation of the colonizer's literature, indigenous production now shows greater diversity and a will to particularize' (Fanon 2004: 172–173). Not only does Wiley depict the tensions within the wider economy, he represents his hustle as affording him protection from those forces. The emphasis on cash in his pocket (and therefore not in the bank) highlights the distance between these social worlds. This signals a movement beyond cathartic expressions of frustration and anger, or tragic images of urban dwelling constructed by Dizzee Rascal or Devlin. Wiley's celebration of hustling foregrounds its political character through its juxtaposition with the financial collapse that struck the city of London.

The changed aesthetic of Wiley's later track can be seen as part of grime artists' explorations of the possibilities available to them in the cultural field. Furthermore, the rising popularity of Funky House, Electro, and other genres indicates a reconfiguration of London's black public sphere. This refashioning does not necessarily indicate the diminished significance of postcodes in young people's political identities. However, tracks such as 'The Swine Flu Skank' and Lethal Bizzle's 'Keys to the Bentley' do not employ grime's 'dark' aesthetic. They suggest a modified approach to the issues confronted in black popular culture. Nevertheless, to assume the hyperbolic materialism of songs such as 'Keys to the Bentley' to be positive, as opposed to grime's apparent 'negativity,' would be mistaken. Such songs build upon the same cultural tradition, even though they may attempt to fashion a different set of responses to urban life. The thematisation of status conferring possessions such as Bentley cars and Rolex watches produces new criteria of judgement. However, the ability of such representations to satisfy their audiences' needs remains questionable. In an interview, Skepta recalled:

> I didn't even have a Rolex before I made 'Rolex Sweep' . . . But after this hype I'm gonna sell the Rolex you get what I'm saying 'cause I'm not a Rolex person. But obviously when I was doing the tune everyone was like 'eh, you got a tune called Rolex Sweep and you ain't got a Rolex' and I went out and bought a wicked man one . . . but I don't floss man, I don't floss.[7]

His statement identifies an expectation that he ought to act in life in the manner that he represents himself through rap. This in turn demonstrates how the offering of such representations to his public is part of an ongoing negotiation between the artist and his audience.

Skepta's ambivalent relation to his status purchase suggests that the aspirational values that this luxury item conveys are not only unattainable for his interpretative community but also unsustainable by himself. Nevertheless, Lethal Bizzle's 'Keys to the Bentley,' in which the MC constructs an image of the attraction of female desire through the possession of a set of car keys, follows and positions itself in relation to this aspect of Skepta's earlier offering. It is significant that the car itself is not the subject of Bizzle's track, but rather the *keys* to what this status item represents. Bizzle's references to this luxury English brand conjure ideas of achievement, freedom, and belonging. Cars are valued for their ability to attract women and as fantasies of celebrity. This representation of the consumption of luxury objects responds to the 'American automotive utopianism' that has been 'exported to black communities in other areas of the world, along with the generic versions of political culture that followed the demise of Black Power' (Gilroy 2010: 16–17). Possession of a Bentley, or the social position it connotes, may be even more out of reach to Lethal B's audience than the Rolex that Skepta intended to sell after the 'hype' surrounding his track died down. But the idea conveyed by the poetry of a moving icon of English luxury and wealth reflects a turn from gritty representations of urban life towards consumer culture in order to explore questions about self-worth and social belonging.

The exaggerated 'celebration' through reference to luxury goods is not merely a response to and movement away from the 'dark' sounds of grime. These lyrics also attempt to reshape and reposition the figure of the MC. Distancing themselves from gritty representations of hustling and urban life, these artists use tracks such as 'Keys to the Bentley' and 'Rolex Sweep' to confer upon themselves some of the qualities that those products carry. In the Choong Family's interview on the Urban World podcast, two years prior to Skepta's interview, the group discussed the impact of 'downloading' on the scene. Nutz argued:

> I ain't saying I ain't downloaded before, yeah. But the problem is, yeah, if you download, the mans next door's music and you know that he's struggling he's not gonna be able to move, you understand. So if you invest and go and buy that, even if you don't like man that much, but you like him enough. We helping you out basically. 'Cause its opening up the flood doors. . . . If you wanna make money go invest in someone else that you like, you understand.[8]

Afix makes clear that what they are concerned with is 'helping our economy grow' and producing a 'movement.' The advocation of this strategy suggests the attempt to build something akin to a pyramid scheme. Somewhat undercutting his position, Nutz admitted that he previously downloaded music without paying for it. His admission betrays the limited potential for artists to make substantial amounts of money in a cultural scene where music is freely distributed. His argument that buying music is an investment identifies the structural limitations to economic development. It also attempts to restructure the relation between rap artists and their listeners. In this proposed arrangement the free distribution of music within the black public sphere would give way, in order for producers to better benefit economically from the newly fashioned black investor/consumers. The 'Rolex Sweep' represents the advancement of an alternative strategy to Nutz's appeal. By purchasing the track consumers are able to construct a relation to the luxury goods–bearing MC.

The reference to a luxury watch in 'Rolex Sweep' was not the only aspect of the song's popularity. The accompanying dance allowed a relation to the artwork that earlier grime offerings did not facilitate. Through the movement of the body, as well as the purchase of the track, dancers were able to explore the aspirational identifications conjured by the MC. The 'Swine Flu Skank' contrasts with Lethal Bizzle's offering, and indicates a distinct line of exploration that builds on the 'Rolex Sweep's' dance orientation. It does not pursue the commodity-driven utopianism that the earlier track solicited. Instead, it explores an alternative trajectory through the cultural field. In contrast to the approach advocated by the Choong Family, more egalitarian possibilities may be cultivated through the appropriation of the Department of Health's 'catch it, bin it, kill it' slogan. Released during the 2009–2010 swine flu pandemic, the music video opens with two young black men reading the paper and watching the television news. One of the men begins to draw his friend's attention to a news report of the ease with which the disease may be contracted, before that friend loudly sneezes. After admonishing his companion, the first man exclaims that those around him should be aware of swine flu, before inviting his audience to take appropriate precautions. The refrain 'catch it, bin it, kill it' is accompanied in the music video by the gestures of sneezing, discarding, and washing. The men perform their healthful skank in various settings, including the streets, shops, and a London Underground station. Their performances invoke ideas of hygiene and personal responsibility and connect these ideas with an engagement with contemporary world events and the health of the social whole. The 'Swine Flu' and 'Migraine' skanks use issues of public and private well-being to connect dancing bodies to practices of social being. This circulation of ideas concerning the health of the nation within the black public sphere may allow the cultivation of alternative forms of vernacular identity through bodily performance. Furthermore, the incorporation of the Department of Health's slogan into the black cultural imaginary in nightclubs across the capital contests notions of rap's marginality to British life and produces new principles around which to live together.

I am not suggesting that public health as collective wealth will become a dominant theme within London's black public sphere. However, I wish to draw out the various strategies through which artists explore the concerns of their interpretative communities and through which identification is solicited and produced. I discussed in the previous chapter Afrikan Boy's appropriation and reconfiguration of material from the 'Migraine' skank in the exploration of slave memory. It is also worth considering that his announcement—'I don't have a Hummer, but I get many whips from my old slave master'—suggests a more cautious approach to the construction of identity through status commodities. It also constructs a distinctive relation between the MC and his audience. Although Ty recognised that he did not have the same standing as a doctor or lawyer in the wider society, rappers' shamanic performances play an important role in the organisation of a collective consciousness of social malaise and solicit responses to these complex issues from their audiences. The efforts of Seeker, Wiley, Skepta,

Afrikan Boy, and Ty also draw attention to how the MC's status in the wider society is, in part, constituted through a negotiation between themselves and their audiences.

CULTURAL ENTREPRENEURISM AND THE PURSUIT OF ECONOMIC AUTONOMY

Following on from my interest in Walter Benjamin's discussion of the appropriation of the artwork by audiences in chapter three, I now want to draw on his concept of the aura to engage with MCs and DJs' relations with their work. In 'The Work of Art in the Age of Mechanical Reproduction,' Benjamin directs his attention to the relation of the artwork to the socioeconomic conditions of its production. With the effect of growing global economic inequalities on social relations in postcolonial London, rappers' attempts to transform their relation to their audiences can be seen as an effort to restore the aura of their artistic production. This process entails the transformation of themselves as economic agents. Benjamin notes that by reducing the actor to a prop, stripped of his aura, '[n]othing more strikingly shows that art has left the realm of the "beautiful semblance" which, so far, had been taken to be the only sphere where art could thrive' (2007: 230). I argue that by taking responsibility for their cultural production MCs and DJs rehabilitate values that are diminished by the relations inscribed in the capitalist mode of production. In so doing these artists resist the erosion of people's freedom to take responsibility for and control of their own lives in contemporary London.

In considering his future JJ informed me that he intended to establish a rave. His plans were ambitious and, even though he was aware that he could get reduced rates from his friends, he expected that he would need to invest about £3,000 to promote the sort of event he was interested in. In preparation for this venture he intended to attend a variety of existing nightclub events to observe how they were organised and would discuss how he might run his own night with club owners and other promoters. In order to develop his awareness of the intricacies of club promotion, he stated, 'I'm looking to get involved with someone else first before I step into my own thing.' Although he saw this step as unnecessary to his ultimate goal of DJing on 'mainstream legal radio, pushing a sound that I like,' he stated that 'for what I want to build as a brand it is very relevant.' He linked the decision to build a brand through nightclub events to a sense of self-worth: 'The money is a factor but only because I don't think its right if someone's capable of something and if they're gonna share that with other people and put a lot of work in—like: pay a man what he's worth innit.' JJ identified that he had developed his self-worth through his expertise as a DJ and radio show host. His decision to build a brand was a shift towards developing greater economic autonomy as a cultural entrepreneur.

The plan to promote his own events held the prospect that JJ would be free to decide the clubs in which they would be held, the other DJs that would play on the night, and how the events would be promoted. It also contained the promise of financial responsibility. 'If that's all in my own hands the only person I can complain to is myself.' The ethic of self-reliance that underlies this reasoning functions as part of a self-fashioning through which he could build upon his cultural inheritance. Having ended his formal education at 16, his work as a DJ provided the means of avoiding 'shit work' in a society that he experiences as racist each time he is stopped by the police. Building a brand through which he is identified is also a method through which he could increase the possibility of acquiring economic wealth. This strategy aims to convert more of the cultural capital that he possesses as a DJ into economic capital. Importantly, it incorporates an ethics of self-worth with the objective of escaping the alienation of the dominant economic relations.

Reain and Rhyme Asylum also make a case for artists being appropriately financially rewarded. Possessed explicitly rejects some hip-hop fans' romantic ideas about their work: 'I don't want bling bling and all that, I want what I deserve. And if they like it . . . they should give me some money. Because it's work, it's still work. Like people think "ah man, you should do it just for the love man."' Their rejection of this idealism was coupled with resistance to the notion that rapping is all about money—'if artists are shit, fuck them, they shouldn't get any money . . . if they are just out for the money, then I agree. Fuck them, they shouldn't get any money.' Reain opposes simplistic views of what it is to be a rapper: 'People are so ignorant to that, they think instantly like hip-hop or rapping "bling bling," "where's your chains?" and all that shit, and I'm like "it doesn't work like that, it's not that simple."' These rappers place an emphasis upon doing a good job and working over the long term. They also reject any notion of gaining rapid success in a moribund scene. In order to justify the value of their work, and their entitlement to expect people to pay for it if they like it, Possessed highlights the labour that has been put into their cultural production:

> All they're seeing is the track. They don't know that I've done some shit job for a year just to pay for studio time and beats or whatever. Or the time I've sat down to get the verse ready. And lets say I wrote a verse in an hour, what about the nine years it's taken me just to get to that level that people actually enjoy it and it's worth listening to.

He also emphasises an emotional investment in the work that highlights an ethical relation to his rapping and through this to his public: 'It's so much going into it and it's your heart and your soul, it's more than money.' His discussion combines an ethics of play and love with a cultural entrepreneurism that places an economic value on the time and care they have invested. These are opposed to the dispiriting relations he and his associates are subject to in the mainstream economy.

Although Possessed and Reain's comments focus on the value of a product in contrast to JJ's emphasis on building a brand, they all emphasise the investments that they have made and the importance of being paid what one is worth. JJ's experience contrasts with that of Possessed in that all of his work is related to music. He teaches music, works in a record shop, and at 18 was able to pay rent and bills at the parental home. Reain and the members of Rhyme Asylum had jobs unrelated to music, through which they funded the production of albums, attendance at shows abroad, and development of the group. JJ's brand-building plans draw attention to his relationship with his labour: 'It does take time to build a brand, because as a DJ you are a brand.' After describing a brand as something that is built over time, he identifies himself with this construction through his work as a DJ. His reasons for wanting to become a promoter in addition to being a DJ do not only connect the prospect of greater control over his work with the goal of receiving just financial remuneration. By identifying himself with a brand he adopts modes of commercial practice in order to enhance his self and its worth. Possessed explicitly justified the commercial value of Rhyme Asylum's products through emphasis on the time, labour, and emotional commitment involved in their cultural production. For these artists the investment of money earned from 'shitty' jobs into a product, through which they express themselves creatively, does not merely compensate them for the socioeconomic position that they occupy. It holds out the possibility of a substantially different relation with their work. By drawing upon their years of practice, or the money that has been spent on equipment, studio time, the experience of DJing to thousands of people, and other achievements, JJ, Reain, and Rhyme Asylum reinvest their MCing and DJing with an aura of human labour. Moving beyond representing their cultural production as a labour of love, the rappers' commercial products and JJ's representation of the DJ as a brand function as a means through which they attempt to receive just financial remuneration for that labour.

In contrast to JJ, who did not attend University, Daz recalls 'juggling' higher education with DJing on pirate radio. He, along with younger artists like Chipmunk, negotiated a balancing act between the formal education system and the informal structures of the 'colony,' in which pirate radio stations are important cultural institutions. Daz's strategy of negotiation between these worlds has developed into a career in IT that still allows him to 'do music every single day.' Contrasting this arrangement with his earlier period of negotiation, he recalls, 'the only thing I done with music back then was play out, buy records and do the radio show. Now there's so much more involved man, so much more. Like preparation for a radio show, interviews in the week, podcasts, mix-tapes, other activities we do, you know what I mean, like working with artists in the studio.' The development of his range of involvement in the music industry is a source of pride for him, but also affords him resilience to changes in the market. During a period in which the performance of grime music in London's nightclubs had been suppressed,

Daz was still able to earn as much money through music as through his employment in the information technology sector: 'I consciously took a decision to step away from the club circuit. A lot of DJs are defined and financed solely from playing out. I stepped away from that and I'm cool. A lot of DJs ask me, "wow, you're doing your thing and I like what you're doing but how do you make money?" I'm like: "I'm making money man."' He sees music as his primary mode of employment, and the ability for his cultural production to fund itself and pay bills is a substantial source of pride.

When his partner decided to focus on his 'day job,' this provided Daz with the challenge of continuing his work as a DJ and host, along with maintaining the prominence of his brand: 'I'm all about challenges, I've never backed down from a challenge.' In particular, Daz considered that having two DJs had given humour to their radio broadcasts—'its good to have that in your show, but I think in the long term my show is not about that anyway. I mean its not about jokes, its not about comedy. And I think sometimes . . . we'd have a little joke with each other, we'd bounce off each other.' The change resulted in a shift in the organisation and tone of the show, but also provided the opportunity for Daz to distinguish himself:

> My show man, its about a person like myself that knows a lot about music and brings that music to the masses, with a lot of information. I keep it quite informative, and I know my music man. A lot of people say they know their music but I do know the music that I'm playing. . . . I think what I'm doing is quite a bit different, and I think a lot of people, will sort of, if they're not doing it now they'll probably be doing it in the future, serious kind of hip-hop DJs. Because I play hip-hop *and* grime. Even though I see grime as the little brother of hip-hop. I play it—hip-hop and grime man—not many DJs do.

By positioning his brand as innovative and informative, Daz fashions himself as a self-sufficient cultural entrepreneur able to offer serious, well-informed commentary on rap music. He considers this work to be more important than his part-time employment in the IT industry. This indicates how this mode of work provides him with something more satisfying than labouring for a salary, regardless of how well qualified his degree makes him for that career. His negotiation of these different modes of economic activity enables him to support his family, and provides the option of falling back on his formal qualifications: 'if this music thing doesn't earn me enough money in the next couple of years you best just believe that I'm gonna work in an office maybe and just get mash—some nice money.' Daz's perseverance in the music industry suggests that the alternative possibility of leaving his office work was more attractive to him. Rather than accept the sort of job that his graduate status opened to him, he maintains his entrepreneurial activities in order to sustain the possibility of living a life that brings his social, cultural, and economic interests together: 'I live this man.'

Artists' investments in their cultural production are part of a process through which they develop a degree of autonomy from the dominant, capitalist, productive relations. This can be seen most acutely in Daz's case, where he has access to well-paid, skilled work in the mainstream economy. JJ in some ways represents the opposite pole of this trend and is more completely immersed in this counterculture. It is significant that his immersion does not require him to become violent (as Anderson's formulation of a 'code of the streets' would have it), because the development of the colony society enables him to earn a stable income, contribute to household bills, and work in a manner consistent with his own interests. His role in the reproduction of colony culture provides some insulation from the forces in the mainstream economy, comparable to that represented in Wiley's 'Cash in my Pocket.'

In a movement that opposes the tendency that Benjamin identified, in which the actor 'offers not only his labour but also his whole self, his heart and soul' (2007: 230) to a market beyond his reach, MCs and DJs transform themselves into brands and personae that are able to reach out to the market, influence it, and receive economic remuneration directly from it. This strategy draws upon the social, cultural, and technological resources of the black public sphere in a refusal of the dominant economic relations. By investing their own money, whether from 'shit' jobs or their cultural production, these artists attempt to rehabilitate the aura of their collective labour. In doing so they adopt some practices from the dominant productive mode, sometimes thinking about themselves in terms that would be applied to commercial organisations. This enables them to direct their labour towards producing art that they love and to gaining a return that they see as justifiable in the light of that labour.

CONCLUSION

Under particular historical conditions, certain social, economic, political, and aesthetic factors may come together. The moment in which 'grime' became an appreciative term and was, subsequently, attached to an emerging musical genre was one such conjuncture. From the embattled position that this subaltern sphere occupies in postcolonial London, it continues to offer resources through which young people come to a consciousness of their relation to the wider society. JJ's comments identify a relation between grime's formal qualities and a 'fast,' 'cheap' mode of life. Attempts by him, Wiley, and others to develop autonomy from the exploitative structures of capitalist production may be related to grime's fast tempo, its percussive rhythms, and the MC's rapid lyrical delivery. The hustling represented and practiced in this scene is part of a struggle in which this marginalised, multiracial group negotiates its subordinate position in London's social and economic structures.

It is important to note that the urban violence represented in some rap lyrics is neither peculiar to grime nor a recent development in London. In a city marred by an immense social and economic chasm, experiences of poverty and the lack of decent public services are more significant causal factors of the violent protection of access to scarce resources and social capital. When considering 'inappropriate' or 'negative' lyrics, it is important to bear in mind that this cultural form is rooted in the lives of London's young inhabitants and that the forces that come to bear upon their everyday lives also impact upon their modes of expression. Depictions of hustling and local particularism represent strategies adopted by urban youths in response to the conditions in which they dwell. The production of these cultural representations for sale is, consequently, a politically significant means of escaping poverty and reliance on the state.

Despite the potential pitfalls of some of the strategies employed by London's marginalised youths, these strategies need to be placed in the context of growing social and economic inequalities. Rhyme Asylum, Reain, and JJ's activities represent developments of the street culture strategy of adopting the 'business mind' to which F refers. Even Seeker's opposition to writing lyrics principally for sale, which is linked to his position as a 'conscious' rapper, is made possible by the alternate means of economic subsistence available to him through local government. These artists' collective efforts reconfigure the position of the MC and DJ in contemporary London. They are also part of a struggle over the economic character of the black public sphere. The construction of identity through aspirations of possessing status objects differs from the investment of the aura of human labour in one's work. Although both strategies highlight the incorporation of mainstream values and practices into contemporary black culture, they construct distinct relations between the artist and audience through that work. Nevertheless, the responses of listeners and dancers to artists' representations of themselves demonstrate how what it means to be an MC or DJ is negotiated with their publics. It is through the interaction between artists and their audiences that relations within London's black public sphere are reworked and that the tone and rhythm of their lives in this city are produced.

NOTES

1. 'Cultural production distinguishes itself from the production of the most common object in that it must produce not only the object in its materiality, but also the value of this object, that is, the recognition of artistic legitimacy' (Bourdieu 1993: 164).
2. http://opac.yale.edu/news/article.aspx?id=6458 [Date Accessed 15 February 2011].
3. http://www.lambeth.gov.uk/Services/EducationLearning/SchoolsColleges/Runn ingOutOfSpaceWillYourChildHaveSchoolPlace2015.htm [Date Accessed 31 May 2011].

4. http://www.southlondonpress.co.uk/news.cfm?id=13561 [Date Accessed 31 May 2011].
5. The identity of this artist is not revealed in order to maintain his/her anonymity.
6. http://www.djsemtex.com/blog/2010/01/08/giggs-nme-interview/ [Date Accessed 23 June 2010].
7. http://urbanworld.co.uk/podcasts/ [Release Date: 1 July 2010].
8. http://urbanworld.co.uk/podcasts/ [Release Date: 1 July 2010].

Conclusion
'Take Back the Scene'

Rap music plays a distinctive role in the everyday lives of London's youths. This oral-poetic form provides a means through which young inhabitants of the city come together to practice and develop their creative and expressive abilities. It also enables a politically significant group of working-class Londoners to resist economic exploitation and develop a greater degree of control over their lives, through their organisation of London's rap music scenes. I have aimed to highlight the depth of black culture in this city, using rap as a point of entry into the ordinary lives of young people. For over 35 years this oral tradition has enabled black and white working-class youths to affirm their common interests and identities. One of the important ways in which they adapt this tradition is through the process of combining orality with the technological resources available to them in London. The use of the Internet, DVDs, podcasts, mobile phones, and music plays an important part in the production of an alternative public sphere in which the interests and identities of young Londoners may be shared, negotiated, and promoted. The playing of black music on the city's public buses is indicative of the mainstream position that this culture now occupies, and of how rap has enabled urban youths to claim public space as their own.

While hip-hop and grime are clearly valued by London's youths as part of their everyday lives, the passions that rap music arouses have also been mobilised at strategic moments in challenges to the moral authority of the nation's political elite. The impromptu 'rave' in Parliament Square during student protests in 2010, against the tripling of University tuition fees and cuts to the Education Maintenance Allowance, was one such moment. The protests were triggered by the coalition government's adoption of the Browne Review, which had been commissioned by the previous Labour government. The potential impact of Lord Browne's (2010) recommendation to remove the cap on tuition fees altogether was somewhat attenuated by the Conservative-Liberal Democrat government's decision to set a £9,000 limit. Paul Mason described one particular scene in these protests:

> Young men, mainly black, grabbed each other around the head and formed a surging dance to the digital beat lit, as the light failed, by the

distinctly analog light of a bench they had set on fire. . . . While a good half of the march was undergraduates from the most militant college occupations—UCL, SOAS, Leeds, Sussex—the really stunning phenomenon, politically, was the presence of youth: *banlieue*-style youth from Croydon, Peckam [*sic*], the council estates of Islington.[1]

The playing of grime tracks, such as Lethal B's 'Pow!,' during protests against government cuts to education-spending highlights how this music provides valuable resources for marginalised groups to challenge the legitimacy of the government's actions. The coalition's programme did more than accelerate the marketisation of the education system in the United Kingdom (by almost tripling the cost to students of higher education) and increase the economic burden placed upon English youths, by withdrawing the Education Maintenance Allowance. It also exacerbated the disconnection between urban youths and party politics. Every Liberal Democrat MP in the coalition government had previously pledged to vote against any increase in tuition fees. They now collectively reneged on those pledges.

As the Browne Review had been commissioned by Labour and implemented by the Conservative and Liberal Democrat parties, further and higher education students were left without the support of any mainstream political party. The convergence of the three largest parliamentary parties around a neoliberal position on public service–spending cuts and an entirely instrumental view of the value of education signal the damaging effects of the managerialism that has come to pervade British politics and the absence of legitimate political choice for the nation's youth in the aftermath of the 2008 financial crisis. Social commentators predicted that the impact of the coalition's cuts on youth services would lead to increased crime and violence, and the National Council for Voluntary Youth Services warned that the cumulative effect of the spending cuts meant that a generation faced diminished public support for their welfare and greater uncertainty about their futures.[2]

In August 2011 riots erupted in London and spread to cities across England. The disorder began after a peaceful protest against the killing of Mark Duggan by the metropolitan police. Despite the timing and context of the riots, MPs from both the governing and opposition parties rushed to characterise the riots as devoid of any political basis. Amidst the clamour to condemn the rioters, David Starkey announced, on the BBC's *Newsnight* programme, that black culture was responsible for the looting and violence spectacularly displayed on television broadcasts of the events. Starkey made clear that his argument was based on Enoch Powell's 'River's of Blood' speech. However, he distinguished himself from Powell by shifting lines of difference that he saw as inevitably leading to violence from biological race to racialised culture: '[T]his is the enormously important thing—it's not skin colour, it's culture':

The whites have become black. A particular sort of violent, destructive, nihilistic gangster culture has become the fashion. And black and white, boy and girl operate in this language together. This language, which is wholly false, which is a Jamaican patois that's been intruded in England.[3]

Starkey then moved on to single out rap for special censure as glorifying riot. His attempt to invoke a myth of white English superiority is an important reminder of the lingering effects of the loss of empire on the nation's political consciousness. England was cast as a victim to the postcolonial migration of culturally inferior blacks. His suggestion that rap music was a causal factor in the riots that had spread across the nation underscores the need to attend to how this cultural form has provided critical reflections on the contemporary British racism that is a legacy of imperial and colonial power. It is also important to note that Starkey was not concerned about violence between ethnic groups, but that this culture provided common ground for different groups to come together. Nevertheless, England was figured as having fallen victim to the presence of formerly colonised people. This interpretation needs to be countered, and a clearer account of the events that led to the widespread disorder advanced. Furthermore, the melancholic longing for a mythically homogenous England, from which Starkey's spurious assertions sprang, demonstrates the necessity of highlighting the value of rap in unsettling ideas of fixed racial identity and producing strategies through which to live with difference as an ordinary feature of metropolitan life.

On August 4, 2011, Mark Duggan was shot dead by police officers in Tottenham. Amid inaccurate information, suggesting an exchange of fire, being given to the press by the Independent Police Complaints Commission, conflicting accounts of the killing circulated. Two days later members of the community, including Duggan's family, marched from the Broadwater Farm estate to Tottenham police station. The protest came to an end peacefully, but without the family having had substantial discussions with senior officers about the events surrounding the killing. Later in the evening, violence broke out in Tottenham, with petrol bombs thrown at police officers and patrol cars set alight. In the days that followed, looting and violence spread across London and then to cities across England. Although the events surrounding the killing of Mark Duggan precipitated the outbreak of violence in Tottenham, numerous reports identified the police's use of 'stop and search' powers as a substantial source of grievance and a motivating factor in the disorder across the country (Riots Communities and Victims Panel 2012: 24).

During the course of the research for this book several rap artists predicted an outbreak of violence. However, neither they nor any of the reports commissioned by the government following the riots suggested that rap might be a causal factor for this violence. Indeed, there was significant agreement between the various reports and one artist's concern that discontent with the legitimacy of the policing of young people in the capital would lead to a violent rejection of authority. The Metropolitan Police Service (MPS) uses stop and search powers twice as often as all but one other police force in England

and Wales, but the number of searches that result in an arrest by the metropolitan police falls below the 9% average across all forces. The report by Her Majesty's Inspectorate of Constabulary (HMIC) into the use of 'stop and search' states that for 'decades the inappropriate use of these powers, both real and perceived, has tarnished the relationship between constables and the communities they serve, and in doing so has brought into question the very legitimacy of the police service' (HMIC 2013: 3). Although 'stop and search' was not an immediate 'cause' for the breakdown of civil order in Tottenham, it may have been a significant factor in the spread of violence.

The authors of *The Guardian* and London School of Economics and Political Science (LSE) report into the England riots argue that for many rioters, 'the spark was the shooting of Mark Duggan in Tottenham. To them, it symbolised the most extreme end of a spectrum of targeted, unjust and brutal treatment to which they perceive they are subjected' (Lewis et al. 2011: 18). We have already seen how grime has been used by young people to externalise the emotions produced by experiences of unjust policing. The association of the poor white and black youths in London's 'street culture' is one of the most significant features of the grime and UK hip-hop scenes, through which these groups represent their social and economic marginalisation. However, those who have repeatedly witnessed or been subject to demeaning and unjustified searches by the police also learn to distrust their authority. HMIC states:

> Of the 8,783 stop and search records we examined, 27% did not include sufficient grounds to justify the lawful use of the power. The reasons for this include low levels of understanding of what constitutes reasonable grounds, poor supervision, and an absence of oversight by senior officers.
>
> (HMIC 2013: 8)

The lack of justification for the use of this intrusive power, as well as the embarrassment that it caused, was commented on by a number of rap artists. HMIC also highlights that police forces have developed approaches to the use of this power that run counter to the stipulation in the 'Code of Practice for the exercise by police officers of statutory powers of stop and search' that '[e]*very reasonable effort must be made to minimise the embarrassment that a person being searched may experience*' (2013: 30, emphasis in text). While poverty was clearly a significant factor in the disorder, with rioters coming 'from the most deprived 20% of areas in the UK' (Lewis et al. 2011), discriminatory policing practices were also a source of antipathy towards the metropolitan police. With unemployment among those young black men who were available for work in 2011 rising to over 50%, the discriminatory and illegitimate use of this power during the years of deep financial crisis would have exacerbated tensions between the police and economically marginalised youths.

The Equalities and Human Rights Commission states that, under legislation requiring reasonable grounds for suspicion, black people nationwide were stopped six times as often as whites (EHRC 2010: 5). However, the discriminatory use of stop and search under section 60 of the Criminal Justice and Public Order Act, which does not require the officer conducting the search to have reasonable grounds for suspicion, was much higher in London. Black people were stopped more than 10 times as often as whites through the use of this power (EHRC 2012: 24). The use of stop and search by the police is most frequently aimed at finding drugs, even though blacks use drugs at a similar or lower level to the white population (Eastwood, Shiner, and Bear 2013: 15). While the use of this power based on a generalised belief that blacks are more likely to commit a crime is unlawful, the discriminatory practice results in the criminalisation of young black people who experience harsher outcomes than their white counterparts. The unlawful use of stop and search, in a manner that causes embarrassment to those subject to the power and that leads to the criminalisation of a disproportionately large number of black urban youths, must be seen as a continuation of the institutional racism that Macpherson found operating in the MPS following the death of Stephen Lawrence in 1993.

Although the riots of 2011 have become lodged in the nation's consciousness, this was also the year in which the Lewisham community commemorated the 30th anniversary of the New Cross fire, in which 13 teenagers died at a house party, following what was widely believed to be a racist arson attack. In North London the death of Joy Gardner at the hands of immigration officers, who had bound her head with 13 feet of tape but were nevertheless found not guilty of manslaughter, formed a part of the Tottenham community's historical memory of injustice. On August 6, following the circulation of conflicting accounts of the shooting, the grime MC Scorcher tweeted, '25 years ago police killed my grandma in her house in Tottenham and the whole ends rioted, 25 years on and they're still keepin up fuckry.' Alongside the killing of Mark Duggan, the historical memory of deaths in police custody, failures to properly investigate the deaths of young black people, and the experience of racially discriminatory treatment by the police combined to produce an eruption of violence. Although Prime Minister David Cameron rushed to label the rioting as criminality 'pure and simple,' his politically expedient comments ignored the community protest and other events that preceded the breakout of rebellion in London. I want to suggest that the breakdown of peaceful protest is a result of the disconnection between substantial proportions of socially and economically marginalised people and mainstream political institutions. Without any faith in the political system, those who took to the streets had little investment in legally sanctioned forms of dissent.

These problems are not unique to England. Similar violence following deaths involving the police has also erupted in France and Sweden in recent years. The riots that consumed Paris in 2005 followed the deaths of two boys who had been chased by police into a power station. Although the police had abandoned the site by the time the one surviving boy rescaled the wall out of the power station, radio transcripts reveal that the police (who failed to contact the power station company, EDF) demonstrated a callous disregard for the boys' lives:

> I think they are about to enter the EDF . . . site; we need reinforcements to surround the neighborhood, or they are going to get out.
> Yes, message received.
> On second thought, if they entered the EDF site, their skin is worth nothing now.
>
> (Quoted in Schneider 2008: 135)

Days later, rioting broke out, spreading from suburb to suburb, 'affecting more than three hundred towns' and lasting 'three convulsive weeks' (Schneider 2008: 136). The Swedish riots in 2013 began in Husby after police killed a 69-year-old man. 'The police reported that he died from injuries in a hospital, but Husby residents had photographed the police removing the dead body from the apartment in the middle of the night' (Back et al. 2013). These incidents of police abuse are exacerbated by experiences of poverty and poor housing. Back et al. (2013) argue that when 'the police shoot an inhabitant in a stigmatized area, it can easily be experienced as an officially sanctioned violation that also symbolizes all of the violations that the inhabitants have suffered for years and in silence.' Increased social inequalities, resulting from neoliberal economic policies in France, Sweden, and the United Kingdom, combined with abusive and discriminatory policing practices are a common feature of the background to these riots.

Far from igniting or glorifying riot, rap artists in France, Sweden, and Britain have produced work that challenges the unemployment and social inequality produced by neoliberal policies. Timbuktu's song 'Ett Brev' (The Letter), released in 2003, challenged the Swedish prime minister to resist adopting the approach of the United States to welfare. This followed a turn away from the inclusive social citizenship of the Swedish model during the 1990s:

> [T]he concurrent neoliberal trend in economic policy, welfare and labour market regulation, anti-discrimination legislation and diversity management that have come to operate in social circumstances that, step by step, are becoming increasingly similar to the structurally based forms of social polarisation, poverty and racialised exclusion that obtain in countries such as the US and the UK.
>
> (Schierup and Ålund 2011: 50)

Whereas the Swedish integration policy of the 1970s had been based on an equitable welfare system and the protection of immigrants' legal rights, the neoliberalisation of the Swedish labour market and the erosion of the welfare state have produced increased poverty amongst the immigrant community. 'In the city of Malmö, almost every third child grows up in poverty. Several satellite towns in Stockholm, Gothenburg and Malmö have child poverty rates above 40 per cent' (Schierup and Ålund 2011: 52). The Swedish pattern of segregation, with gentrified city centres and impoverished satellite towns, bears similarities to the subjection of marginalised youths to poor education and dilapidated housing provision in French *Banlieues* (Schneider 2008: 143; Haddad and Balz 2006: 27–28). It is towards this background of racism and neoliberalisation that these riots should direct our attention.

By examining two of London's rap music scenes in detail, this book has sought to contribute to a history of everyday multiculturality and to contribute to the exploration of alternative projections of the future from those dominated by American race politics. The local narratives of living with difference present within the UK hip-hop and grime scenes may prove valuable in the cultivation of European identities that are suspicious of fabricated ideas of cultural homogeneity. They may also enable the process of working through the legacy of colonisation and fear of the other expressed by figures such as Starkey. Rap plays an important role in constructing patterns of identification, which trouble the categories that supply the defenders of mythical national homogeneity with their bogus certainties of white superiority. The collective production of a common culture and interracial identification through rap music provide opportunities for strengthening our democratic institutions and challenging racism across Europe. Rappers' challenges of the inadequacies of contemporary politics in addressing the impact of racism, social and economic inequality, and the production of substantive forms of inclusive citizenship need to be supplemented by critical engagement with the production of subaltern identities and alternative publics through these artists' work. The articulation of race and class in critical representations of the state of Europe's nations needs to be considered as an important contribution to the development of European pluralism.

NOTES

1. http://www.bbc.co.uk/blogs/newsnight/paulmason/2010/12/9122010_dubstep_rebellion_-_br.html [Date Accessed 9 October 2013].
2. http://www.ncvys.org.uk/blogs.php?act=view_topic&id=204 [Date Accessed 9 October 2013].
3. http://www.bbc.co.uk/news/uk-14513517 [Date Accessed 29 August 2011].

Discography

Afrikan Boy (2010) 'Lidl' *Yes We Can* Outhere Records
———(2012) 'Kunta Kinte' *Kunta Kinte/Eba Eater* Melted Dubs
———'Afrikan Boy 3Style 4Captian TB TV' YouTube [Date Accessed 5 October 2011]
Bashy (2009) 'Black Boys' *Catch Me If You Can* Ragz2Richez
Devlin (2010) 'Community Outcast' *Bud, Sweat and Beers* Universal Records
Dizzee Rascal (2003) 'I Luv U' *Boy In Da Corner* XL Recordings
———(2007) 'Sirens' *Maths + English* XL Recordings
Durrty Goodz (2007) 'Switching Songs 2' *Axiom* Awkward Music
Gracious K (2009) 'Migraine Skank' *Migraine Skank* Sony Music
Lethal Bizzle 'Keys to the Bentley' YouTube [Date Accessed 5 October 2011]
Mavado (2007) 'Squeeze Breast' *Gangsta for Life* VP Records
MC Nobody 'Jerusalem' YouTube [Date Accessed 5 October 2011]
No. Lay 'Unorthodox Daughter' YouTube [Date Accessed 5 October 2011]
Rihanna (2009) 'Hard' *Rated R* Def Jam
Roll Deep (2007) 'Roll Deep Regular' *Rules and Regulations* Roll Deep
Roots Manuva (2001) 'Witness (1 Hope)' *Run Come Save Me* Big Dada
Sincere (2008) 'Once Upon a Time' *Once Upon a Time (ft. Natty)* Ye-Records
Skepta (2011) 'Rolex Sweep' *Microphone Champion* Boy Better Know
Sticky (2001) 'Booo!' *Booo! (ft. Ms Dynamite)* Social Circles
Tiny Wides, R2k, Baby Fusion 'Grime Online Freestyle' GrimeOnline.co.uk [Date Accessed 11 July 2008]
Uproar Unlimited 'Swine Flu Skank' YouTube [Date Accessed 5 October 2011]
Wiley (2004) 'Wot Do U Call It' *Treddin' On Thin Ice* XL Recordings
———(2008) 'Cash in My Pocket' *See Clear Now* Warner Music

Bibliography

Abrahams, R. (1972) 'Joking: The Training of the Man of Words in Talking Broad' in Thomas Kochman (ed.) *Rappin' and Stylin' Out* Urbana, IL: University of Illinois Press, pp. 215–240
—— (1993) 'Playing the Dozens' in Alan Dundes (ed.) *Mother Wit From The Laughing Barrel* Jackson: University Press of Mississippi, pp. 295–309
Anderson, E. (2000) *Code of the Street* New York: Norton
Arnold, M. (2006) *Culture and Anarchy* Oxford: Oxford University Press
Austin, J. L. (1976) *How to Do Things with Words* London: Oxford University Press
Back, L., Gilroy, P., Dikec, M., Listerborn, C., Molina, I., Sernhede, O., . . . Vradis, A. (2013) 'Husby and Territorial Stigma in Sweden's Open Democracy.' https://www.opendemocracy.net/les-back-paul-gilroy-others-see-below/husby-and-territorial-stigma-in-sweden [Date Accessed 10 June 2013].
Baker, H. A. (1996) 'Critical Memory and the Black Public Sphere' in The Black Public Sphere Collective (eds) *The Black Public Sphere* Chicago: University of Chicago Press, pp. 7–37
Bakhtin, M. (1984) *Rabelais and His World* (trans. Helene Iswolsky) Bloomington, IN: Indiana University Press
Benjamin, W. (2007) *Illuminations* New York: Random House
Bennett, A. (1999) 'Rappin' on the Tyne: White Hip Hop Culture in Northeast England' *The Sociological Review* Vol. 47, No. 1: 1–24
Bey, H. (1985) 'The Temporary Autonomous Zone, Ontological Anarchy, Poetic Terrorism' New York: Autonomedia. http://hermetic.com/bey/taz_cont.html [Date Accessed 10 September 2010].
Bradley, A. (2009) *Book of Rhymes: The Poetics of Hip-Hop* New York: Basic Civitas
Brathwaite, E. K. (1984) *History of the Voice* London: New Beacon Books
Brown, H. (1972) 'Street Talk' in Thomas Kochman (ed.) *Rappin' and Stylin' Out* Urbana, IL: University of Illinois Press, pp. 205–208
——(1993) 'Street Smarts' in Alan Dundes (ed.) *Mother Wit From The Laughing Barrel* Jackson: University Press of Mississippi, pp. 353–356
Browne, J. (2010) 'Securing a Sustainable Future for Higher Education: An Independent Review of Higher Education Funding and Student Finance Department for Business, Innovation & Skills. https://www.gov.uk/government/publications/the-browne-report-higher-education-funding-and-student-finance [Date Accessed 8 October 2013].
Bourdieu, P. (1984) *Distinction* (trans. Richard Nice) London: Routledge & Kegan Paul
——(1993) *The Field of Cultural Production* Cambridge: Polity Press
Buck-Morss, S. (1992) 'Aesthetics and Anaesthetics: Walter Benjamin's Artwork Essay Reconsidered' *October* Vol. 62: 3–41

Butler, J. (1999) 'Performativity's Social Magic' in Richard Shusterman (ed.) *Bourdieu: A Critical Reader* Oxford: Blackwell Publishers, pp. 113–128

Chambers, I. (1985) *Urban Rhythms: Pop Music and Popular Culture* Basingstoke, UK: Macmillan

Cooper, C. (1993) *Noises in the Blood* London: Macmillan

Davis, G. (1985) *I Got the Word In Me and I Can Sing It, You Know* Philadelphia: University of Pennsylvania Press

De Nora, T. (1999) 'Music as a Technology of the Self' *Poetics* Vol. 27: 31–56

DuBois, W.E.B. (2000) *The Souls of Black Folk* Chicago: Lushena Books

Eastwood, N., Shiner, M., and Bear, D. (2013) *The Numbers in Black and White: Ethnic Disparities in the Policing and Prosecution of Drug Offences in England and Wales* London: Release

EHRC (2010) *Stop and Think: A Critical Review of the Use of Stop and Search Powers in England and Wales* Manchester: Equality and Human Rights Commission

———(2012) *Race Disproportionality in Stops and Searches Under Section 60 of the Criminal Justice and Public Order Act 1994* Manchester: Equality and Human Rights Commission

Ellison, R. (1995) 'Twentieth-Century Fiction and the Black Mask of Humanity' in *Shadow and Act* New York: Vintage International, pp. 24–44

Fanon, F. (2004) *The Wretched of the Earth* (trans. Richard Philcox) New York: Grove Press

———(2007) *Black Skin, White Masks* (trans. Richard Philcox) New York: Grove Press

Gilroy, P. (1994) ' "After the Love Has Gone": Bio-Politics and Etho-Poetics in the Black Public Sphere' *Public Culture* Vol. 7: 49–76

———(1999) 'A London Sumtin Dis . . . ' *Critical Quarterly* Vol. 41, No. 3: 57–69

———(2002) *There Ain't No Black in the Union Jack* London: Routledge

———(2010) *Darker Than Blue* Cambridge, MA: Belknap Press

GLA (2008a) *Way to Go* London: Greater London Authority

Habermas, J. (1989) *The Structural Transformation of the Public Sphere* Cambridge: Polity

Haddad, Y. and Balz, M. (2006) 'The October Riots in France: A Failed Immigration Policy or the Empire Strikes Back?' *International Migration* Vol. 44, No. 2: 23–24

Hall, S. (2012) *City, Street and Citizen: The Measure of the Ordinary* London: Routledge

Hall, S., Critcher, C., Jefferson, T., Clarke, J., and Roberts, B. (1978) *Policing the Crisis* London: Macmillan

Heathcott, J. (2003) 'Urban Spaces and Working-Class Expressions Across the Black Atlantic: Tracing the Routes of Ska' *Radical History Review* Vol. 87: 183–206

Hebdige, D. (1993) *Cut 'N' Mix* London: Routledge

Hesmondhalgh, D. and Melville, C. (2001) 'Urban Breakbeat Culture: Repercussions of Hip-Hop in the United Kingdom' in Tony Mitchell (ed.) *Global Noise: Rap and Hip-Hop Outside the USA* Middletown, CT: Weslyan University Press, pp. 86–110

Hewitt, R. (1986) *White Talk Black Talk: Inter-Racial Friendship and Communication Amongst Adolescents* Cambridge: Cambridge University Press

HMIC (2013) *Stop and Search Powers: Are the Police Using Them Effectively and Fairly?* Her Majesty's Inspectorate of Constabulary

Johnson, L.K. (1976) 'Jamaican rebel music' *Race & Class* Vol. 17: 397–412

Kim, H. (2012) 'A "Desi" Diaspora? The Production of "Desiness" and London's Asian Urban Music Scene' *Identities: Global Studies in Culture and Power* Vol. 19, No. 5: 557–575

Krims, A. (2000) *Rap Music and the Poetics of Identity* Cambridge: Cambridge University Press

Kohl, H. and Hinton, J. (1972) 'Names, Graffitti and Culture' in Thomas Kochman (ed.) *Rappin' and Stylin' Out* Urbana, IL: University of Illinois Press, pp. 109–133

Lefebvre, H. (1991) *The Production of Space* (trans. Donald Nicholson-Smith) Oxford: Blackwell

Lewis, P., Newburn, T., Taylor, M., Mcgillivray, C., Greenhill, A., Frayman, H., and Proctor, R. (2011) *Reading the Riots: Investigating England's Summer of Disorder* London: The London School of Economics and Political Science and The Guardian

MacCabe, C., Ali, M., Carlin, P., Gilroy, P., Hext, K., Kureishi, H., . . . Young, S. (2006) 'Multiculturalism after 7/7: A CQ Seminar' *Critical Quarterly* Vol. 48, No. 2: 1–44

Miller, D. (1991) 'Absolute Freedom in Trinidad' *Man* Vol. 26, No. 2: 323–341

Mitchell, T. (2001) 'Introduction: Another Root—Hip-Hop Outside the USA' in Tony Mitchell (ed.) *Global Noise: Rap and Hip-Hop Outside the USA* Middletown, CT: Weslyan University Press, pp. 1–38

Mitchell-Kernan, C. (1972) 'Signifying, Loud-Talking, and Marking' in Thomas Kochman (ed.) *Rappin' and Stylin' Out* Urbana, IL: University of Illinois Press, pp. 315–335

Ong, W. (2002) *Orality and Literacy* London: Routledge

Potter, R. A. (1995) *Spectacular Vernaculars* Albany: State University of New York Press

Riots Communities and Victims Panel (2012) *After the Riots: The Final Report of the Riots Communities and Victims Panel* London: The Riots Communities and Victims Panel

Rose, T. (1994) *Black Noise* Hanover, NH: Wesleyan University Press and University Press of New England

Schierup, C. and Ålund, A. (2011) 'The End of Swedish Exceptionalism? Citizenship, Neoliberalism and the Politics of Exclusion' *Race & Class* Vol. 53: 45–64

Schneider, C. (2008) 'Police Power and Race Riots in Paris' *Politics & Society* Vol. 36: 133–159

Shusterman, R. (1991) 'The Fine Art of Rap' *New Literary History* Vol. 22, No. 3: 613–632

Small, C. (1987) *Music of the Common Tongue* London: Calder

Stewart, S. (1978) *Nonsense* Baltimore: Johns Hopkins University Press

Stuckey, S. (1987) *Slave Culture* New York: Oxford University Press

Taussig, M. (1987) *Shamanism, Colonialism, and the Wild Man* Chicago: The University of Chicago Press

Thornton, S. (1995) *Club Cultures* Cambridge: Polity Press

Voloshinov, V. N. (1973) *Marxism and the Philosophy of Language* (trans. Ladislav Matejka and I. R. Titunik) New York: Seminar Press

Wakeford, N. (2003) 'Research Note: Working with New Media's Cultural Intermediaries' *Information, Communication & Society* Vol. 6, No. 2: 229–245

West, C. (1992) 'An Interview with Cornel West' in Peter Brooker (ed.) *Modernism / Postmodernism* London: New York: Longman, pp. 213–224

———(1993) *Race Matters* Boston: Beacon Press

Willis, P. (1990) *Common Culture* Boulder, CO: Westview

Witkin, R. and De Nora, T. (1997) 'Aesthetic Materials and Aesthetic Agency' *Newsletter of the Sociology of Culture Section of the American Sociological Association* Vol. 12, No. 1: 1–6

Wright, R. (1989) 'How Bigger Was Born' in *Native Son* New York: Harper Perennial, pp. vvi–xxxiv

————(2008) 'The Literature of the Negro in the United States' in Cornel West (ed.) *Black Power* New York: Harper Collins, pp. 729–773

RADIO PROGRAMMES

On the Top Deck, Jolyon Jenkins Producer, [Broadcast on BBC Radio 4 on Wednesday, 21 January 2009, 11:00]

TV PROGRAMMES

Friday Night with Jonathan Ross, BBC One, [Broadcast on 30 April 2010]

WEBSITE RESOURCES

BBC (2007) http://news.bbc.co.uk/1/hi/uk/6938411.stm [Date Accessed 2010]
BBC (2008a) http://news.bbc.co.uk/1/hi/uk/7395875.stm [Date Accessed 2010]
BBC (2008b) http://news.bbc.co.uk/1/hi/uk/7777963.stm [Date Accessed 2010]
BBC (2008c) http://news.bbc.co.uk/1/hi/uk_politics/7503845.stm [Date Accessed 2010]
BBC (2010) http://news.bbc.co.uk/1/hi/world/europe/8447990.stm [Date Accessed 2010]
DJ Semtex (2010) http://www.djsemtex.com/blog/2010/01/08/giggs-nme-interview/ [Date Accessed 2010]
GLA (2007a) http://www.london.gov.uk/assembly/assemmtgs/2007/plenarymar14/ item05a.rtf [Date Accessed 2009]
GLA (2007b) http://www.london.gov.uk/assembly/assemmtgs/2007/plenaryfeb14/ minutes/mins-app2.pdf [Date Accessed 2009]
GLA (2008b) http://www.london.gov.uk/assembly/reports/transport/crime-disorder-buses.pdf [Date Accessed 2009]
Guardian (2009) http://www.guardian.co.uk/society/2009/sep/07/met-police-form-696-clubs [Date Accessed 2009]
Guardian (2010) http://www.guardian.co.uk/music/2010/jul/14/wiley-zip-files-free-downloads [Date Accessed 2010]
Lambeth (2011) http://www.lambeth.gov.uk/Services/EducationLearning/Schools Colleges/RunningOutOfSpaceWillYourChildHaveSchoolPlace2015.htm [Date Accessed 2011]
Metropolitan Police Association (2009) http://www.mpa.gov.uk/committees/cep/ 2009/091112/09/?qu=Equalities%20Impact%20Assessment%20696&sc=2& ht=1 [Date Accessed 2010]
Smith, Rodney (2007) http://www.rootsmanuva.co.uk [Date Accessed 2007]
South London Press (2011) http://www.southlondonpress.co.uk/news.cfm?id=13561 [Date Accessed 2011]
The Sun (2008) http://www.thesun.co.uk/sol/homepage/news/justice/1519825/After-12-hours-of-gangsta-rap-I-could-have-knifed-someone.html [Date Accessed 2010]
The Sun (2009a) http://www.thesun.co.uk/sol/homepage/news/2396038/Defoe-brother-dies-after-street-attack.html [Date Accessed 2010]
The Sun (2009b) http://www.thesun.co.uk/sol/homepage/news/2402448/Defoe-brother-suspect-appears-in-court.html [Date Accessed 2010]
Yale University (2009) http://opac.yale.edu/news/article.aspx?id=6458 [Date Accessed 2011]

Index